I0009360

© [2025] Evan Rhodes

All rights reserved. No part of this book may be reproduced, in any form or by any means, including electronic, mechanical, photocopying, recording, or otherwise, without the prior written permission of the publisher, except for brief excerpts used in reviews.

Disclaimer: The information contained in this book is for educational purposes only. While every effort has been made to ensure the accuracy of the content, the author and publisher disclaim any responsibility for errors or omissions. Readers are encouraged to seek professional advice where needed.

THE COMPLETE LUA PROGRAMMING GUIDE

*Create Games, Apps, and Scripts
with Hands-On Projects*

By

Evan Rhodes

Contents

3

Introduction

Why Learn Lua?

Lua is a lightweight, high-performance programming language that has carved out a unique niche in the programming world. Whether you're a game developer, a systems engineer, or just starting your programming journey, **Lua** offers a simplicity and versatility that makes it an attractive choice.

At its core, **Lua** is:

1. **Simple and Beginner-Friendly:** With a clean syntax and minimal setup, **Lua** is easy to learn, even for those new to programming.
2. **Lightweight but Powerful:** Lua's efficient runtime makes it ideal for

performance-critical applications like games, embedded systems, and mobile apps.

3. **Extensible: Lua** was designed to be integrated with other programming languages, making it a go-to scripting language for engines like Unity, Roblox, and Love2D.

For instance, if you've played a game that uses Roblox or tinkered with software that uses scripting, there's a high chance **Lua** was working behind the scenes. Even Adobe Lightroom employs **Lua** to manage its powerful automation features.

If you're passionate about building games, automating tasks, or working with hardware, **Lua** is a great skill to add to your toolkit.

Key Features and Applications of Lua

What makes **Lua** stand out? Let's explore some of its most notable features and real-world applications.

1. **Lightweight Architecture**
   Lua has a tiny memory footprint, which makes it ideal for embedding in systems with limited resources. For example, **Lua** is often used in IoT devices to run scripts efficiently.

Powerful Table System
Tables in **Lua** function as arrays, dictionaries, or objects. This single, flexible data structure simplifies programming.

9

lua

```lua
-- Example of a Lua table as an array
local fruits = {"apple", "banana", "cherry"}
for i, fruit in ipairs(fruits) do
    print("Fruit:", fruit)
end

-- Output:
-- Fruit: apple
-- Fruit: banana
-- Fruit: cherry
```

2. This versatility helps developers solve a wide range of problems without learning multiple data types.
3. **Coroutines for Parallel Execution**
   Coroutines in **Lua** allow efficient

multitasking, perfect for handling asynchronous tasks like animations in games or network operations.

4. **Embedded Usage**
   Lua is widely used in:
   - **Game Development:** Engines like Love2D and Roblox Studio rely heavily on **Lua** scripting.
   - **Embedded Systems: Lua** scripts run on microcontrollers and other embedded platforms.
   - **Task Automation: Lua** scripts automate repetitive tasks, saving time and effort.

5. **Ease of Integration**
   Lua can work seamlessly with C, C++, and other programming languages. This makes it an excellent choice for adding

scripting capabilities to existing applications.

How to Use This Book

This book is structured to take you from the fundamentals of **Lua** to advanced applications, with a focus on hands-on learning. Each chapter builds on the previous one, offering clear explanations, practical examples, and interactive projects.

Key Highlights:

- **Step-by-Step Learning**: We'll start with **Lua** basics and gradually introduce advanced topics like coroutines, debugging, and game development.
- **Practical Projects**: Every chapter ends with a hands-on project that

applies the concepts covered, ensuring you learn by doing.

- **Real-World Applications:** We'll explore how **Lua** is used in game development, automation, and IoT, so you can see its relevance firsthand.
- **Downloadable Resources:** Sample scripts and project templates will be available for you to experiment with and customize.

For example, at the end of the chapter on **Lua** basics, you'll create a **number guessing game:**

lua
```
-- Number Guessing Game
local secret = math.random(1,
100) -- Generate a random
number between 1 and 100
local guess = nil
```

```lua
print("Welcome to the Lua
Number Guessing Game!")
print("Try to guess the number
I'm thinking of (1-100).")

while guess ~= secret do
    io.write("Enter        your
guess: ")
    guess                       =
tonumber(io.read())

    if guess < secret then
        print("Too  low!  Try
again.")
    elseif guess > secret then
        print("Too  high!  Try
again.")
    else

print("Congratulations!    You
guessed it!")
    end
```

```
end
```

This small project is a glimpse of the kind of interactive learning you'll experience throughout the book.

By the end of this journey, you'll not only have mastered **Lua** but also gained confidence to build your own applications, games, and automation scripts. Let's dive in and start unlocking the power of **Lua**!

Chapter 1: Getting Started with Lua

Lua is a fantastic programming language for beginners and professionals alike, thanks to its simplicity and versatility. This chapter will guide you through setting up your **Lua** environment, writing your first script, and understanding the fundamental syntax and rules. By the end, you'll even build a simple calculator script!

1.1 Installing Lua and Setting Up the Environment

Before diving into **Lua** programming, we need to set up an environment where you can write and execute **Lua** scripts. This process is straightforward, and by the end of this section, you'll be ready to start coding.

Step 1: Download Lua

The first step is to download **Lua** for your operating system. Here's how to do it:

1. **Go to the Official Lua Website**
   Visit www.lua.org and navigate to the **Download** section.
2. **Select the Latest Version**
   Choose the most recent stable release (e.g., **Lua** 5.4.x).

Step 2: Install Lua

Follow the instructions for your operating system:

For Windows Users:

1. **Download the Lua for Windows Package**
   - You can download a precompiled binary from a community-supported source like **Lua**Binaries or use Windows Subsystem for Linux (WSL) for a Unix-like experience.

2. **Install Lua**
   - Run the installer and follow the on-screen prompts.
   - Ensure the `bin` directory is added to your system's PATH variable so **Lua** can be accessed from the Command Prompt.

3. **Verify Installation**

Open the Command Prompt and type: bash

```
lua -v
```

You should see something like:

```
Lua 5.4.x
```

o

For macOS Users:

1. **Use Homebrew**
   If you haven't already, install
   Homebrew, a popular package
   manager for macOS.

Install Lua via Homebrew
Open Terminal and run:
bash

```
brew install lua
```

2.

3. **Verify Installation**

Check the **Lua** version by typing:
bash

```
lua -v
```

○

For Linux Users:

1. **Install Using a Package Manager**
   Most Linux distributions include **Lua** in their repositories. Use the following commands based on your distro:

Ubuntu/Debian:
bash

```
sudo apt-get install lua5.4
```

○

Fedora:

bash

```
sudo dnf install lua
```

       o

2. **Verify Installation**

Check   **Lua**'s   installation   with:
bash

```
lua -v
```

       o

Step 3: Setting Up an Editor

While you can write **Lua** scripts in any text editor, using an editor with syntax highlighting and debugging features can make development easier.

- Recommended Editors:
  - Visual Studio Code: Lightweight, customizable, and supports **Lua** extensions.
  - Notepad++: Great for simple script editing on Windows.
  - Sublime Text: A powerful editor with **Lua** syntax highlighting.

Setting Up Visual Studio Code for Lua

1. Install Visual Studio Code.
2. Open the Extensions Marketplace and search for "**Lua**". Install the **Lua Language Server** extension.
3. Create a new **Lua** file (`.lua`) and start coding!

Step 4: Running Lua Scripts

Once **Lua** is installed, you can start running scripts.

Method 1: Direct Execution in the Terminal

1. Open a terminal or command prompt.

Enter **Lua**'s interactive mode by typing: bash

```
lua
```

Test by typing:
lua

```
print("Hello, Lua!")
```

You should see:

```
Hello, Lua!
```

Method 2: Running Lua Files

1. Create a new file called `test.lua`.

Add the following code:
lua

```
print("Welcome to Lua programming!")
```

Save the file and run it in the terminal using:
bash

```
lua test.lua
```

Output:
css

```
Welcome to Lua programming!
```

Step 5: Online Lua Editors (Optional)

If you're not ready to install **Lua** on your system, online editors like Replit or OneCompiler allow you to write and execute **Lua** scripts in your browser.

For example, you can run the following script online to check **Lua**'s functionality:

lua

```
-- Simple Lua script

local name = "Developer"

print("Hello, " .. name .. "!
Welcome to Lua.")
```

This outputs:

css

```
Hello, Developer! Welcome to
Lua.
```

1.2 Writing Your First Lua Script

Now that **Lua** is installed, it's time to get your hands dirty by writing your very first **Lua** script. Writing a script is simple, but understanding what's happening behind the scenes will help you build a solid foundation. Let's take it step by step.

Step 1: Create a Lua File

1. Open your preferred text editor (e.g., Visual Studio Code, Notepad++, or Sublime Text).

2. Create a new file and save it as
   `first_script.`**`lua`**.
   - Ensure the file extension is
     `.lua` to indicate that it's a
     Lua script.

Step 2: Write Your Script

For your first script, let's print a friendly message to the console.

Code Example:

lua

```
-- This is your first Lua
script

-- The print() function is used
to display text in the console
```

```lua
print("Hello, Lua World!")
```

Step 3: Run Your Script

1. Open your terminal or command prompt.

Navigate to the folder where `first_script.lua` is saved. For example:
bash

```bash
cd path/to/your/file
```

Run the script using the **Lua** interpreter:
bash
```bash
lua first_script.lua
```

You should see the following output:

```
Hello, Lua World!
```

Congratulations! You've just written and executed your first **Lua** script.

Understanding the Code

Let's break down the script:

1. **Comments**
   - Comments in **Lua** start with -- for single lines or --[[...]] for multi-line comments.
   - These are ignored by the **Lua** interpreter and used to document your code.
2. **The** `print()` **Function**

- The `print()` function outputs text or values to the console.
- In this example, `print("Hello, Lua World!")` tells **Lua** to display the string `"Hello, Lua World!"`.

Enhancing Your Script

Now let's add some interactivity by asking the user for their name and greeting them.

Code Example:

lua

```
-- This script greets the user
with a personalized message
```

```lua
-- Prompt the user for their
name

io.write("What is your name?
") -- Use io.write() to print
without a newline

local name = io.read()
-- Read user input and store it
in the variable 'name'



-- Display a personalized
greeting

print("Hello, " .. name .. "!
Welcome to Lua programming.")
```

Running the Script:

1. Save the script and run it in the
   terminal as before.

When prompted, enter your name.
csharp

```
What is your name? Alex
```

The script will output:
css

```
Hello, Alex! Welcome to Lua
programming.
```

Explanation of the Enhanced Script

1. **The `io.write()` Function**
   - Similar to `print()`, but it doesn't add a newline at the end, allowing you to format prompts neatly.

2. **The `io.read()` Function**
   - This function captures user input from the console.
   - In this script, the user's input is stored in the variable `name`.

3. **String Concatenation**
   - **Lua** uses `..` to concatenate (combine) strings.

For example:

lua

```
"Hello, " .. name .. "!"
```

   - Combines `"Hello, "`, the user-provided `name`, and `"!"` into one string.

Expanding Further: A Simple Math Script

Let's make things a bit more dynamic by writing a script that performs basic math operations.

Code Example:

lua

```
-- Simple Math Script


-- Ask the user for two numbers
io.write("Enter    the    first
number: ")

local         num1          =
tonumber(io.read())         --
Convert input to a number
```

```lua
io.write("Enter    the    second
number: ")

local          num2          =
tonumber(io.read())          --
Convert input to a number


-- Perform basic operations

print("The sum of the numbers
is: " .. (num1 + num2))

print("The difference of the
numbers is: " .. (num1 - num2))

print("The  product  of  the
numbers is: " .. (num1 * num2))


-- Handle division carefully
```

```
if num2 ~= 0 then

    print("The quotient of the
numbers is: " .. (num1 / num2))

else

    print("Division by zero is
not allowed!")

end
```

Running the Script:

1. Save and execute the script.

Input two numbers when prompted.
mathematica

```
Enter the first number: 10

Enter the second number: 5
```

The output will display the results:
python

```
The sum of the numbers is: 15

The difference of the numbers
is: 5

The product of the numbers is:
50

The quotient of the numbers is:
2
```

1.3 Understanding Lua Syntax and Rules

Lua's simplicity and readability are among its most appealing features. In this chapter, we'll break down the key aspects of **Lua** syntax and rules, laying a strong foundation for your programming journey. By the end, you'll feel confident about writing clean and effective **Lua** code.

Case Sensitivity

Lua is case-sensitive. This means `Variable`, `variable`, and `VARIABLE` are treated as distinct identifiers.

Example:

lua

```
local Variable = 10
local variable = 20
```

```
print(Variable)    -- Outputs:
10

print(variable)    -- Outputs:
20
```

Comments

Comments are essential for making your code readable and maintainable. **Lua** supports two types of comments:

- **Single-line comments:** Use --.
- **Multi-line comments:** Use --[[and]].

Example:

lua

```lua
-- This is a single-line comment

--[[

This is a multi-line comment.

It can span several lines.

]]
```

Variables

Variables in **Lua** are dynamically typed, meaning you don't need to declare their type explicitly. You simply use the `local` keyword to define them.

Rules for Variable Names:

1. Must begin with a letter (A-Z or a-z).
2. Can include letters, digits, and underscores (_).
3. Cannot be a reserved keyword (e.g., `if`, `then`, `end`).

Example:

lua

```
local name = "Alex"    -- A string

local age = 25         -- An integer

local height = 5.9     -- A floating-point number


print(name, age, height)
```

Data Types

Lua supports several basic data types:

1. **Nil:** Represents the absence of a value.
2. **Boolean:** `true` or `false`.
3. **Number:** Represents numeric values (both integers and floats).
4. **String:** A sequence of characters enclosed in quotes.
5. **Table: Lua**'s only complex data structure, used for arrays, dictionaries, and objects.
6. **Function:** Represents executable code.

Example:

lua

```lua
local isStudent = true    --
Boolean

local score = nil         -- Nil

local grade = 98.5        --
Number

local greeting = "Hello, Lua!"
-- String
```

Operators

Arithmetic   **Operators:**
Lua supports standard arithmetic operations.

lua

```
local a, b = 10, 5


print(a + b)   -- Addition: 15

print(a - b)   -- Subtraction:
5

print(a    *    b)          --
Multiplication: 50

print(a / b)   -- Division: 2

print(a % b)   -- Modulus: 0

print(a    ^    b)          --
Exponentiation: 100000
```

Relational Operators:
These return `true` or `false` based on
comparisons.

lua

```lua
local x, y = 10, 20

print(x < y)   -- true
print(x > y)   -- false
print(x == y) -- false
print(x ~= y)  -- true (not equal)
```

Logical Operators:
Used for Boolean logic.

lua

```lua
local isAdult = true
```

```lua
local hasLicense = false


print(isAdult and hasLicense)
-- false

print(isAdult or hasLicense)
-- true

print(not isAdult)          -
- false
```

Control Structures

Lua provides standard control structures for decision-making and loops.

If-Else Statements:

lua

```lua
local age = 18

if age >= 18 then
    print("You are an adult.")
else
    print("You are a minor.")
end
```

For Loop:

lua

```lua
for i = 1, 5 do
    print("Count: " .. i)
```

```
end
```

While Loop:

lua

```lua
local count = 1

while count <= 5 do
    print("Count: " .. count)
    count = count + 1
end
```

Functions

Functions in **Lua** are first-class citizens, meaning they can be assigned to variables and passed as arguments.

Defining and Calling Functions:

lua

```
local function greet(name)

    print("Hello, " .. name ..
"!")

end



greet("Lua Programmer")    --
Outputs:     Hello,     Lua
Programmer!
```

Anonymous Functions:

lua

```lua
local add = function(a, b)
    return a + b
end
print(add(10, 5))  -- Outputs: 15
```

Tables

Tables are the cornerstone of **Lua** programming, functioning as arrays, dictionaries, or objects.

Example: Array-like Table

lua

```lua
local    fruits   =    {"apple",
"banana", "cherry"}

for i, fruit in ipairs(fruits)
do

    print(i, fruit)

end
```

Example: Key-Value Table

lua

```lua
local person = {

    name = "Alex",

    age = 30,

    profession = "Developer"

}
```

```lua
print(person.name)        --
Outputs: Alex
```

Hands-On Example: Simple Script Using Syntax Rules

Let's put everything together in a single script:

Code Example:

lua

```lua
-- Define a function to
calculate the area of a
rectangle

local            function
calculateArea(length, width)

    return length * width
```

```lua
end


-- Get user input

io.write("Enter the length: ")

local        length       =
tonumber(io.read())        --
Convert input to number


io.write("Enter the width: ")

local        width        =
tonumber(io.read())        --
Convert input to number

-- Calculate and display the
area

local        area         =
calculateArea(length, width)
```

```lua
print("The    area    of    the
rectangle is: " .. area)
```

Running the Script:

1. Save the script as
   `area_calculator.`**`lua`**.

Run it in the terminal and provide the required   inputs.
yaml

```
Enter the length: 10

Enter the width: 5

The area of the rectangle is:
50
```

Hands-On Project: Building a Basic Calculator Script

Let's take what we've learned about **Lua** and create something functional: a basic calculator script. This project will reinforce key programming concepts while producing a handy tool you can expand later.

Step 1: Setting the Goal

The calculator will allow users to:

1. Perform basic arithmetic operations: addition, subtraction, multiplication, and division.
2. Handle invalid inputs gracefully.
3. Exit the program when they're done.

Step 2: The Blueprint

Our calculator will:

1. Display a menu of options.
2. Accept user input for the operation and numbers.
3. Perform the calculation based on the chosen operation.
4. Loop until the user decides to exit.

Step 3: Writing the Code

Here's the complete code for your calculator:

lua

```
-- Basic Calculator Script
```

```lua
-- This program performs basic
arithmetic operations based on
user input


-- Function to display the menu

local function displayMenu()

    print("\nBasic
Calculator")

    print("1. Addition")

    print("2. Subtraction")

    print("3. Multiplication")

    print("4. Division")

    print("5. Exit")

    io.write("Choose an option
(1-5): ")
```

```lua
end


-- Function to perform the
chosen operation
local             function
performOperation(option, num1,
num2)
    if option == 1 then
        return num1 + num2,
"Addition"
    elseif option == 2 then
        return num1 - num2,
"Subtraction"
    elseif option == 3 then
        return num1 * num2,
"Multiplication"
```

```lua
    elseif option == 4 then

        if num2 == 0 then

            return           nil,
"Error: Division by zero is not
allowed."

        end

        return  num1  /  num2,
"Division"

    else

        return  nil,  "Invalid
operation."

    end
end


-- Main program loop
```

```lua
while true do

    displayMenu()  -- Show the
menu

    local        choice        =
tonumber(io.read())   -- Read
the user's choice


    if choice == 5 then
        print("Exiting     the
calculator. Goodbye!")
        break
    end


    if choice < 1 or choice >
5 then
```

```lua
        print("Invalid choice.
Please    select    a    valid
option.")

    else

        -- Get numbers from
the user

        io.write("Enter    the
first number: ")

        local    num1    =
tonumber(io.read())


        io.write("Enter    the
second number: ")

        local    num2    =
tonumber(io.read())
```

```lua
    -- Perform the
calculation
    local result, message
=    performOperation(choice,
num1, num2)


    if result then
        print(message .. "
result: " .. result)
    else
        print(message)
    end
  end
end
```

Step 4: Testing the Script

Run the script by saving it as `calculator.lua` and executing it in the terminal:
bash

```
lua calculator.lua
```

1.

The menu will appear:
markdown

```
Basic Calculator

1. Addition

2. Subtraction

3. Multiplication

4. Division
```

```
5. Exit

Choose an option (1-5):
```

2.
3. Select an option and follow the prompts to enter numbers.
4. The script will output the result or an error message (e.g., for division by zero).

Code Explanation

1. **Display Menu Function (`displayMenu`)**
   - This function prints the menu options and prompts the user to select one.
2. **Operation Function (`performOperation`)**

- Performs the arithmetic operation based on the user's choice.
- Includes error handling for division by zero.

3. **Main Loop**
   - Keeps the program running until the user selects option 5 (Exit).
   - Validates user input and ensures the program handles invalid choices gracefully.

Enhancements You Can Add Later

1. **Support for More Operations**
   - Include operations like modulus (%) or exponentiation (^).
2. **Repeat Calculations Without Exiting**

- Allow users to perform multiple calculations before returning to the main menu.

3. **Input Validation**
   - Ensure users enter valid numbers and handle non-numeric inputs elegantly.

4. **Enhanced Interface**
   - Improve user interaction with more descriptive prompts or even colors (if using a terminal that supports it).

Sample Output

Here's an example of how the program behaves:

markdown

Basic Calculator

1. Addition

2. Subtraction

3. Multiplication

4. Division

5. Exit

Choose an option (1-5): 1

Enter the first number: 15

Enter the second number: 5

Addition result: 20

Basic Calculator

1. Addition

2. Subtraction

3. Multiplication

4. Division

5. Exit

Choose an option (1-5): 4

Enter the first number: 10

Enter the second number: 0

Error: Division by zero is not allowed.

Basic Calculator

1. Addition

2. Subtraction

3. Multiplication

4. Division

5. Exit

Choose an option (1-5): 5

Exiting the calculator. Goodbye!

Chapter 2: Lua Basics – Variables and Control Structures

Understanding the basics of variables, control structures, and functions is critical for writing effective **Lua** programs. In this chapter, we will delve into these fundamental concepts to set a strong foundation for your programming journey.

2.1 Variables, Data Types, and Operators

Understanding variables, data types, and operators is fundamental when working with **Lua** or any programming language. **Lua** keeps these concepts straightforward, making it an excellent language for beginners and professionals alike.

Variables in Lua

A **variable** is a named storage for data, and in **Lua,** variables are dynamically typed. This means a variable can hold any type of value without needing to declare its type explicitly.

To create a variable, you simply assign a value to a name using the = operator. By default, variables are **global,** but it's good practice to use `local` to limit their scope.

Example: Declaring Variables

lua

```
local greeting = "Hello, Lua!"
-- A string variable
```

```
local age = 25          -
- A number variable

local isLearning = true     -
- A boolean variable
```

```
print(greeting)    --    Output:
Hello, Lua!
```

Data Types in Lua

Lua supports a few basic data types:

1. **Nil:** Represents the absence of a value (default value of uninitialized variables).
2. **Boolean:** Can be `true` or `false`.
3. **Number:** Represents both integers and floating-point numbers.

4. **String**: A sequence of characters enclosed in quotes.
5. **Function:** Represents executable code.
6. **Table: Lua**'s single, flexible data structure for arrays, dictionaries, or objects.
7. **Thread** and **Userdata:** More advanced types for specific uses.

Example: Working with Different Data Types

lua

```
local score = 100         -
- Number

local playerName = "Alex"   -
- String

local isActive = true      -
- Boolean
```

```lua
local details = nil          -
- Nil
```

```lua
print(type(score))           -
- Output: number
```

```lua
print(type(playerName))      -
- Output: string
```

```lua
print(type(isActive))        -
- Output: boolean
```

```lua
print(type(details))         -
- Output: nil
```

Operators in Lua

Operators are used to perform operations on variables and values. **Lua** provides a variety of operators for arithmetic, relational, and logical operations.

Arithmetic Operators

Used to perform mathematical calculations:

- + (Addition)
- - (Subtraction)
- * (Multiplication)
- / (Division)
- % (Modulus)
- ^ (Exponentiation)

Example: Using Arithmetic Operators

lua

```
local a, b = 10, 3

print(a + b)   -- Output: 13

print(a - b)   -- Output: 7
```

```
print(a * b)    -- Output: 30

print(a  /  b)      --  Output:
3.3333333333333

print(a % b)   -- Output: 1

print(a ^ b)   -- Output: 1000
```

Relational Operators

These compare two values and return
true or false:

- < (Less than)
- > (Greater than)
- <= (Less than or equal to)
- >= (Greater than or equal to)
- == (Equal to)
- ~= (Not equal to)

Example: Relational Operators

lua

```
local x, y = 5, 10

print(x < y)    -- Output: true

print(x >= y)  -- Output: false

print(x == y)  -- Output: false

print(x ~= y)   -- Output: true
```

Logical Operators

These are used to perform Boolean logic:

- and (Logical AND)
- or (Logical OR)
- not (Logical NOT)

Example: Logical Operators

lua

```lua
local isSunny = true

local isWarm = false


print(isSunny and isWarm)   -- Output: false

print(isSunny or isWarm)    -- Output: true

print(not isSunny)          -- Output: false
```

Best Practices with Variables and Operators

Use **meaningful variable names** to make your code self-explanatory.
lua

```lua
local studentName = "Alice" --
Clear and descriptive
```

1.
2. **Initialize variables** before use to avoid unexpected results.
3. **Prefer local variables** to avoid polluting the global scope.

Be mindful of operator precedence. Use parentheses for clarity if needed.
lua

```lua
local result = 5 + 2 * 3 --
Result is 11 (multiplication
has higher precedence)

local clearResult = (5 + 2) *
3 -- Result is 21
```

Hands-On Example: Calculating the Area of a Circle

Let's put these concepts into practice by writing a **Lua** script to calculate the area of a circle based on user input.

Code Implementation

lua

```
-- Program to calculate the
area of a circle


-- Define the value of pi

local pi = 3.14159
```

```lua
-- Prompt the user for the radius

io.write("Enter the radius of the circle: ")

local radius = tonumber(io.read()) -- Convert input to a number


-- Calculate the area using the formula: area = pi * r^2

local area = pi * radius ^ 2


-- Display the result

print("The area of the circle with radius " .. radius .. " is: " .. area)
```

Code Explanation

1. **Input:** The program uses `io.read()` to accept the radius from the user and `tonumber()` to ensure it's treated as a number.
2. **Processing:** The formula for the area of a circle is applied: `pi * radius^2`.
3. **Output:** The result is concatenated with strings and printed.

Sample Output

arduino

```
Enter the radius of the circle:
5

The  area  of  the  circle  with
radius 5 is: 78.53975
```

2.2 Conditional Statements and Loops

In programming, decision-making and repetition are essential for building dynamic applications. **Lua** offers simple yet powerful constructs for conditional statements and loops, enabling you to control the flow of your programs effectively.

Conditional Statements in Lua

Conditional statements allow your program to make decisions based on certain conditions. **Lua** supports the following conditional structures:

- `if`

- if...else
- if...elseif...else
- nested if

The Basic `if` Statement

The `if` statement evaluates a condition, and if it's true, the associated block of code is executed.

Syntax:

lua

```
if condition then

    -- Code to execute if
condition is true

end
```

Example:

lua

```lua
local temperature = 30

if temperature > 25 then
    print("It's a warm day!")
end
```

---

if...else Statement

Adds an alternate block of code to execute if the condition is false.

Syntax:

lua

```lua
if condition then
    -- Code to execute if condition is true
else
    -- Code to execute if condition is false
end
```

Example:

lua

```lua
local time = 18

if time < 12 then
```

```lua
    print("Good morning!")
else
    print("Good evening!")
end
```

---

if...elseif...else Statement

Used for multiple conditions.

Syntax:

lua

```lua
if condition1 then
    -- Code for condition1
```

```lua
elseif condition2 then

    -- Code for condition2

else

    -- Code if none of the
conditions are true

end
```

Example:

lua

```lua
local score = 85


if score >= 90 then

    print("Grade: A")
```

```lua
elseif score >= 80 then
    print("Grade: B")
else
    print("Grade: C")
end
```

Nested if Statements

An if statement inside another if.

Example:

lua

```lua
local age = 20
local hasPermission = true
```

```
if age >= 18 then

    if hasPermission then

        print("You         can
enter.")

    else

        print("You         need
permission to enter.")

    end

else

    print("You are too young
to enter.")

end
```

Loops in Lua

Loops are used to execute a block of code repeatedly. **Lua** provides three types of loops:

1. `while` Loop
2. `for` Loop
3. `repeat...until` Loop

`while` Loop

Repeats as long as the condition remains true.

Syntax:

lua

```
while condition do
    -- Code to execute
```

```
end
```

Example:

lua

```lua
local count = 1

while count <= 5 do
    print("Count: " .. count)
    count = count + 1
end
```

---

for Loop

Used when the number of iterations is known.

Syntax:

lua

```
for variable = start, stop,
step do

    -- Code to execute

end
```

Example:

lua

```
for i = 1, 5 do

    print("Iteration: " .. i)
```

```
end
```

Custom Step Example:

lua

```
for i = 10, 1, -2 do
    print("Countdown: " .. i)
end
```

---

repeat...until Loop

Similar to a while loop but guarantees at least one execution as the condition is checked at the end.

Syntax:

lua

```
repeat
```

```lua
    -- Code to execute
until condition
```

Example:

lua

```lua
local number = 1
repeat
    print("Number:    "    .. number)
    number = number + 1
until number > 3
```

Practical Example: Checking Odd or Even Numbers

This example combines conditional statements and loops.

Code Implementation:

lua

```lua
-- Ask the user for a range
io.write("Enter the starting number: ")
local startNum = tonumber(io.read())


io.write("Enter the ending number: ")
local endNum = tonumber(io.read())


-- Iterate through the range
```

```
for i = startNum, endNum do

    if i % 2 == 0 then

        print(i    ..    "    is
even.")

    else

        print(i .. " is odd.")

    end

end
```

Explanation:

1. **Input:** The user specifies a range.
2. **Loop:** The program iterates through each number.
3. **Condition:** A number is classified as even or odd using the modulus operator (%).

Sample Output:

csharp

Enter the starting number: 1

Enter the ending number: 5

1 is odd.

2 is even.

3 is odd.

4 is even.

5 is odd.

2.3 Functions and Scope

Functions are the building blocks of reusable and modular code in **Lua**. They allow you to encapsulate logic, making your code more efficient, readable, and maintainable. In this chapter, we'll explore functions in **Lua**, their syntax, how to define and call them, and the concept of scope.

What Are Functions?

A function is a block of reusable code designed to perform a specific task. Functions can:

- Simplify complex programs.
- Avoid repetition by allowing code reuse.

- Make your programs more readable.

Defining and Calling Functions

Functions in **Lua** are defined using the `function` keyword. Once defined, you can call the function to execute the code within it.

Syntax for Defining a Function:

lua

```
function
functionName(parameters)

    -- Code to execute

    return result

end
```

Calling a Function:

lua

```
functionName(arguments)
```

Example: A Simple Greeting Function

lua

```
-- Define the function
function greet(name)
    print("Hello, " .. name ..
"! Welcome to Lua
programming.")
end
```

```lua
-- Call the function

greet("Alice")

greet("Bob")
```

Explanation:

1. **Definition:** The `greet` function takes one parameter, `name`.
2. **Concatenation:** `..` is used to join strings.
3. **Execution:** The function is called with different arguments (`"Alice"` and `"Bob"`).

Output:

css

```
Hello, Alice! Welcome to **Lua** programming.
```

```
Hello, Bob! Welcome to Lua
programming.
```

Functions with Return Values

A function can return a result to the calling code using the `return` keyword.

Example: Adding Two Numbers

lua

```
-- Define the function

function addNumbers(a, b)

    return a + b

end
```

```lua
-- Call the function and store
the result

local result = addNumbers(5,
7)

print("The sum is: " .. result)
```

Output:

python

```
The sum is: 12
```

Anonymous Functions

In **Lua,** functions can be defined without a name. These are called anonymous functions and are often used as arguments to other functions.

Example: Anonymous Function

lua

```lua
-- Using an anonymous function
with table.sort

local numbers = {5, 3, 8, 1}

table.sort(numbers,
function(a, b) return a < b
end)


-- Print sorted numbers

for _, num in ipairs(numbers)
do

    print(num)
```

```
```

```
1

3

5

8
```

Understanding Scope in Lua

Scope refers to the visibility and lifetime of variables. **Lua** has two types of scopes:

1. **Global Scope:** Variables are accessible from anywhere in the program.
2. **Local Scope:** Variables are accessible only within the block where they are defined.

Global Variables

By default, variables in **Lua** are global. However, excessive use of global variables can lead to unpredictable behavior and bugs.

Example:

lua

```
x = 10  -- Global variable
```

```
function printX()

    print(x)    -- Accessible
here

end



printX()

print(x)   -- Accessible here
too
```

Local Variables

Local variables are created using the
`local` keyword. They are preferable for
avoiding conflicts and improving
performance.

Example:

lua

```lua
function calculateSquare(number)
    local result = number * number  -- Local variable
    return result
end

print(calculateSquare(4))
-- print(result) -- This would cause an error as 'result' is local
```

Combining Functions and Scope

Let's create a simple calculator using functions and demonstrate the use of local and global variables.

Code Example:

lua

```lua
-- Global variable

operation = "Addition"


-- Define a function

function calculator(a, b)

    local result

    if operation == "Addition" then
```

```
        result = a + b

    elseif    operation    ==
"Subtraction" then

        result = a - b

    else

        result = "Unsupported
operation"

    end

    return result

end


-- Perform addition

print(calculator(5,  3))    --
Output: 8
```

```lua
-- Change the operation and
perform subtraction

operation = "Subtraction"

print(calculator(10, 4))    --
Output: 6
```

Hands-On Example: Creating a Factorial Function

Let's write a function to calculate the factorial of a number.

Code Implementation:

lua

```lua
-- Define the factorial
function
```

```
function factorial(n)

    if n == 0 then

        return 1

    else

        return n * factorial(n
- 1)

    end

end


-- Test the function

print("Factorial of 5: " ..
factorial(5))  -- Output: 120

print("Factorial of 7: " ..
factorial(7))  -- Output: 5040
```

Explanation:

1. **Base Case:** When n is 0, the factorial is 1.
2. **Recursive Case:** Calls itself with n - 1 until the base case is reached.

Hands-On Project: "Creating a Number Guessing Game"

Let's put everything we've learned so far into practice by creating an interactive number guessing game in **Lua**. This project will use variables, conditional statements, loops, and functions to build a fun and engaging game.

Project Overview

The goal of this game is simple: the program generates a random number, and the player has to guess it. For every incorrect guess, the game provides feedback to help the player get closer to the correct answer.

Step-by-Step Guide

Step 1: Set Up the Game Environment

To make the game dynamic, we need a way to generate random numbers. **Lua** provides a built-in function for this: `math.random()`.

lua

```
-- Seed the random number generator for unique results each time

math.randomseed(os.time())
```

Step 2: Generate a Random Number

We'll generate a random number between 1 and 100 for the player to guess.

lua

```lua
-- Generate a random number between 1 and 100
local secretNumber = math.random(1, 100)
```

Step 3: Create a Function for the Game Logic

To keep the code clean, we'll encapsulate the game logic in a function.

lua

```lua
-- Function to start the
guessing game

function playGame()
    local guess = nil  -- To
store the player's guess

    local attempts = 0 -- To
track the number of attempts


    print("Welcome to the
Number Guessing Game!")

    print("I have selected a
number between 1 and 100. Can
you guess it?")
```

```lua
    -- Game loop
    repeat
        io.write("Enter  your
guess: ")
        guess                =
tonumber(io.read()) -- Convert
input to a number
        attempts = attempts +
1


        -- Provide feedback
        if       guess       <
secretNumber then
            print("Too    low!
Try again.")
        elseif   guess       >
secretNumber then
```

```
        print("Too   high!
Try again.")

        else


print("Congratulations! You've
guessed  the  number  in  "  ..
attempts .. " attempts.")

        end

    until       guess       ==
secretNumber

end
```

Step 4: Handle Edge Cases

To make the game user-friendly, we'll add checks for invalid inputs.

lua

```lua
-- Enhanced input validation
function playGame()
    local guess = nil
    local attempts = 0

    print("Welcome    to    the
Number Guessing Game!")
    print("I  have  selected  a
number between 1 and 100. Can
you guess it?")

    repeat
```

```lua
    io.write("Enter    your
guess: ")

    guess = io.read()


    -- Validate input
    if not tonumber(guess)
then
        print("Please
enter a valid number!")
    else
        guess           =
tonumber(guess)
        attempts        =
attempts + 1
```

```lua
        if    guess    <
secretNumber then

            print("Too
low! Try again.")

            elseif   guess   >
secretNumber then

            print("Too
high! Try again.")

        else


print("Congratulations! You've
guessed the number in " ..
attempts .. " attempts.")

        end

    end

  until    guess    ==
secretNumber
```

```lua
end
```

Step 5: Replay Option

Let's allow the player to replay the game without restarting the program.

lua

```lua
-- Function to play again
function startGame()
    while true do
        playGame()
        io.write("Would    you
like  to  play  again? (yes/no):
")
```

```lua
        local    response    =
io.read():lower()

        if  response  ~=  "yes"
then

            print("Thanks  for
playing! Goodbye!")

            break

        else

            -- Generate  a  new
number for the next round

            secretNumber     =
math.random(1, 100)

        end

    end

end
```

Complete Code

Here's the full code for the number guessing game:

lua

```lua
-- Seed the random number generator
math.randomseed(os.time())


-- Generate a random number
local secretNumber = math.random(1, 100)


-- Function to play the game
```

```lua
function playGame()

    local guess = nil

    local attempts = 0


    print("Welcome to the
Number Guessing Game!")

    print("I have selected a
number between 1 and 100. Can
you guess it?")


    repeat

        io.write("Enter your
guess: ")

        guess = io.read()
```

```
    if not tonumber(guess)
then

        print("Please
enter a valid number!")

    else

        guess           =
tonumber(guess)

        attempts        =
attempts + 1


        if      guess    <
secretNumber then

            print("Too
low! Try again.")

        elseif   guess   >
secretNumber then
```

```lua
            print("Too
high! Try again.")

        else

print("Congratulations! You've
guessed the number in " ..
attempts .. " attempts.")

        end

    end

    until       guess       ==
secretNumber

end


-- Function to start the game

function startGame()

    while true do
```

```lua
        playGame()

        io.write("Would    you
like to play again? (yes/no):
")

        local    response    =
io.read():lower()

        if response ~= "yes"
then

            print("Thanks   for
playing! Goodbye!")

            break

        else

            secretNumber    =
math.random(1, 100)

        end

    end
```

```
end
```

```
-- Start the game
```

```
startGame()
```

What You've Learned

1. **Random Number Generation:** Using `math.random()` to create unpredictable results.
2. **Input Validation:** Ensuring the user provides valid input.
3. **Functions:** Encapsulating logic into reusable blocks.
4. **Loops:** Using `repeat...until` to create an interactive experience.

This project demonstrates the power and simplicity of **Lua**, blending logic and creativity to create an engaging application. As you grow more comfortable, consider enhancing this game by:

- Adding difficulty levels.
- Keeping track of high scores.
- Creating a graphical user interface with **Lua** frameworks.

Chapter 3: Working with Tables – Lua's Core Data Structure

Tables are at the heart of **Lua**. They're versatile, powerful, and serve as **Lua's** only built-in data structure, acting as arrays, dictionaries, and more. Mastering tables is essential for writing efficient and elegant **Lua** programs. This chapter will explore tables in depth, covering their structure, manipulation, and advanced features like metatables and metamethods. By the end, you'll be confident in using tables to solve real-world problems.

3.1 Arrays, Dictionaries, and Nested Tables

Tables are **Lua's** most powerful and flexible data structures, and understanding how to work with them is critical to unlocking **Lua**'s potential. Tables can act as arrays, dictionaries, or even nested structures. In this section, we'll break down these types, explaining how to use them effectively in your programs.

Arrays in Lua

An array is a type of table where keys are sequential integers. **Lua** arrays are particularly useful for handling ordered lists of items.

Creating and Accessing Arrays

To define an array, list its elements in curly braces {}. Access individual elements using their index, starting from 1.

```lua
-- Define an array
local fruits = {"Apple", "Banana", "Cherry"}


-- Access elements
print(fruits[1])  -- Output: Apple


-- Update an element
fruits[2] = "Blueberry"
print(fruits[2])  -- Output: Blueberry
```

Adding and Removing Elements

Lua provides built-in functions to manipulate arrays:

- `table.insert`: Adds an element to a specific position.
- `table.remove`: Removes an element from a specific position.

lua

```
-- Add a new element
table.insert(fruits,
"Dragonfruit")

print(fruits[4])   -- Output:
Dragonfruit
```

```lua
-- Remove an element
table.remove(fruits,   2)   --
Removes "Blueberry"

for i, fruit in ipairs(fruits)
do

    print(i, fruit)
end
```

Iterating Over Arrays

Use `ipairs` for ordered iteration through arrays.

lua

```lua
for    index,    fruit    in
ipairs(fruits) do

    print(index, fruit)
```

```
end
```

Dictionaries in Lua

A dictionary is a table where keys are not sequential integers but instead can be strings, numbers, or other unique values.

Creating and Accessing Dictionaries

Dictionaries allow for more descriptive and meaningful keys.

lua

```lua
-- Define a dictionary
local student = {
    name = "Alice",
```

```
    age = 20,

    grade = "A"

}


-- Access dictionary values

print(student.name) -- Output:
Alice


-- Update a value

student.age = 21

print(student.age) -- Output:
21
```

Adding and Removing Key-Value Pairs

You can easily add or delete keys in a dictionary:

lua

```lua
-- Add a new key-value pair
student.subject = "Mathematics"
print(student.subject) -- Output: Mathematics


-- Remove a key-value pair
student.grade = nil -- Removes the "grade" key
```

Iterating Over Dictionaries

Use `pairs` to iterate over all key-value pairs in a dictionary.

lua

```lua
for   key,   value   in
pairs(student) do

    print(key, value)

end
```

Nested Tables

Lua tables can contain other tables, allowing you to create complex data structures.

Creating a Nested Table

Nested tables can represent hierarchical data, such as a list of students with their details.

lua

```lua
local students = {

    {name = "Alice", age = 20,
grade = "A"},

    {name = "Bob", age = 22,
grade = "B"}

}



-- Access nested table
elements

print(students[1].name)    --
Output: Alice
```

```lua
print(students[2].grade)    --
Output: B
```

Iterating Over Nested Tables

You can combine ipairs or pairs to traverse nested tables.

lua

```lua
for    _,    student    in
ipairs(students) do

    for    key,    value    in
pairs(student) do

        print(key, value)

    end

end
```

Practical Example: Managing Nested Data

Consider a company directory where employees are grouped by departments.

lua

```lua
local company = {
    HR = {
        {name = "Alice", role = "Manager"},
        {name = "John", role = "Recruiter"}
    },
    IT = {
        {name = "Bob", role = "Developer"},
```

```lua
        {name = "Eve", role =
"System Admin"}

    }

}


-- Access specific employee
details

print(company.IT[1].name)    --
Output: Bob


-- Iterate over the company
structure

for department, employees in
pairs(company) do

    print("Department:",
department)
```

```lua
    for    _,    employee    in
ipairs(employees) do
        print("         Name:",
employee.name,    "|    Role:",
employee.role)
    end
end
```

3.2 Metatables and Metamethods

Metatables and metamethods are some of **Lua**'s most advanced and fascinating features. They allow you to customize the behavior of tables, enabling powerful techniques such as operator overloading, custom indexing, and more. In this chapter, we'll explore what metatables and metamethods are, why they are useful, and how to use them effectively.

What are Metatables?

A metatable is a table that defines special behaviors for another table. By attaching a metatable to a regular table, you can override or extend its default functionality.

Creating and Assigning Metatables

You can set a metatable for a table using the `setmetatable` function. The metatable itself is another **Lua** table.

lua

```lua
local myTable = {} -- A regular
table
```

```lua
local meta = {} -- A metatable
```

```lua
-- Set the metatable for
myTable
setmetatable(myTable, meta)
```

To retrieve a table's metatable, use the getmetatable function:

lua

```lua
print(getmetatable(myTable)) -
- Outputs the metatable
reference
```

What are Metamethods?

Metamethods are special keys in a metatable that define specific behaviors for the associated table. These keys usually start with double underscores (__).

For example:

- `__add`: Defines behavior for the + operator.
- `__index`: Customizes behavior when accessing a missing key.
- `__newindex`: Controls what happens when adding a new key-value pair.

Common Metamethods

1. Operator Overloading

Metamethods like __add, __sub, and __mul allow you to define custom behavior for arithmetic operations on tables.

lua

```lua
local vector1 = {x = 2, y = 3}
local vector2 = {x = 4, y = 5}

local meta = {
    __add = function(v1, v2)
        return {x = v1.x + v2.x, y = v1.y + v2.y}
    end
}
```

```lua
setmetatable(vector1, meta)


-- Add the two vectors

local result = vector1 +
vector2

print(result.x, result.y) --
Output: 6 8
```

2. Custom Indexing with `__index`

The `__index` metamethod is triggered when a key is accessed that doesn't exist in the table. You can use it to create default values or link tables.

lua

```lua
local default = {x = 0, y = 0}
local point = {}


setmetatable(point, {__index =
default})


print(point.x) -- Output: 0
print(point.z) -- Output: nil
(since `z` is not in the
default table)
```

You can also set __index to a function:

lua

```lua
setmetatable(point, {
```

```lua
    __index = function(_, key)

        return key .. " is not
defined."

    end

})
```

```lua
print(point.z) -- Output: z is
not defined.
```

3. Controlling New Assignments with __newindex

The __newindex metamethod is triggered when a new key-value pair is added to the table. This is useful for validation or logging changes.

lua

```lua
local restrictedTable = {}
local meta = {
    __newindex = function(_, key, value)
        print("Attempt to add:", key, "=", value)
    end
}

setmetatable(restrictedTable, meta)
```

```
restrictedTable.name = "Lua" -
- Output: Attempt to add: name
= Lua
```

4. Custom Equality with __eq

The __eq metamethod defines custom behavior for the equality operator (==).

lua

```
local obj1 = {id = 1}
local obj2 = {id = 1}


local meta = {
    __eq = function(o1, o2)
        return o1.id == o2.id
```

```lua
        end
}


setmetatable(obj1, meta)

setmetatable(obj2, meta)


print(obj1 == obj2) -- Output:
true
```

Advanced Use Cases

Chaining Metatables

You can create a chain of behaviors by nesting metatables:

lua

```lua
local grandparent = {z = 10}

local parent = {__index =
grandparent}

local child = {}


setmetatable(child, parent)


print(child.z) -- Output: 10
(inherited from grandparent)
```

Tables as Classes

Metatables enable a basic object-oriented
programming approach in **Lua.**

lua

```lua
local Person = {}
Person.__index = Person


function Person:new(name, age)
    return  setmetatable({name
= name, age = age}, self)
end


function Person:info()
    return self.name .. " is "
.. self.age .. " years old."
end
```

```lua
local           alice           =
Person:new("Alice", 25)

print(alice:info()) -- Output:
Alice is 25 years old.
```

Practical Example: Custom Table Behavior

Let's implement a metatable that tracks table accesses and updates.

lua

```lua
local tracker = {}

local meta = {

    __index = function(_, key)
```

```lua
        print("Accessing
key:", key)

        return nil

    end,

    __newindex  =  function(_,
key, value)

        print("Setting  key:",
key, "to", value)

        rawset(tracker,   key,
value) -- Use rawset to bypass
__newindex

    end

}


setmetatable(tracker, meta)
```

```lua
-- Accessing keys

print(tracker.foo) -- Output:
Accessing key: foo


-- Setting keys

tracker.bar = 42 -- Output:
Setting key: bar to 42

print(tracker.bar) -- Output:
42
```

3.3 Practical Examples for Table Manipulation

Tables are the cornerstone of **Lua** programming, serving as arrays, dictionaries, and everything in between.

In this chapter, we'll work through practical examples to demonstrate how to manipulate tables effectively. These examples will help solidify your understanding of **Lua**'s table features while showcasing common scenarios you'll encounter in real-world projects.

Basic Table Operations

1. Adding and Updating Elements

You can add or update elements in a table by assigning a value to a key.

lua

```lua
local fruits = {}


-- Adding elements
```

```
fruits[1] = "Apple"

fruits[2] = "Banana"


-- Updating elements

fruits[1] = "Mango"


-- Printing elements

print(fruits[1])  --  Output:
Mango

print(fruits[2])  --  Output:
Banana
```

2. Removing Elements

To remove an element from a table, set its key to `nil`. This frees up memory associated with that key.

lua

```lua
local fruits = {"Apple", "Banana", "Cherry"}


-- Removing the second element
fruits[2] = nil


-- Printing table
for i, fruit in ipairs(fruits) do
    print(i, fruit)
```

```
end

-- Output:

-- 1 Apple

-- 3 Cherry
```

---

3. Iterating Over a Table

Lua provides two main functions for iterating over tables: `pairs` and `ipairs`.

- **pairs**: Use this for tables with non-numeric keys or mixed key types.
- **ipairs**: Use this for numeric key sequences (arrays).

lua

```lua
local studentGrades = {Math = 85, Science = 90, English = 88}

-- Using pairs
for subject, grade in pairs(studentGrades) do
    print(subject, grade)
end

local numbers = {10, 20, 30, 40}

-- Using ipairs
```

```lua
for      index,      value      in
ipairs(numbers) do

    print(index, value)

end
```

Sorting Tables

Lua doesn't have built-in support for sorting dictionaries, but arrays can be sorted using the `table.sort` function.

lua

```lua
local numbers = {5, 2, 9, 1, 7}


-- Sorting in ascending order
```

```lua
table.sort(numbers)


-- Printing sorted numbers

for _, num in ipairs(numbers) do

    print(num)

end

-- Output: 1 2 5 7 9
```

For custom sorting, provide a comparator function.

lua

```lua
local words = {"Banana", "Apple", "Cherry"}
```

```lua
-- Custom sort by reverse order

table.sort(words,  function(a,
b) return a > b end)


for _, word in ipairs(words) do

    print(word)

end

-- Output: Cherry Banana Apple
```

Nested Tables

Tables can hold other tables as elements, allowing for complex data structures.

lua

```lua
local student = {
    name = "Alice",
    grades = {Math = 90, Science = 85},
    contact = {
        phone = "123-456-7890",
        email = "alice@example.com"
    }
}


-- Accessing nested elements
```

```lua
print(student.name) -- Output:
Alice

print(student.grades.Math)  --
Output: 90

print(student.contact.email) -
- Output: alice@example.com
```

Combining Tables

To merge two tables, you can iterate over one and copy its elements to the other.

lua

```lua
local table1 = {1, 2, 3}

local table2 = {4, 5, 6}
```

```
for _, value in ipairs(table2)
do

    table.insert(table1,
value)

end


for _, value in ipairs(table1)
do

    print(value)

end

-- Output: 1 2 3 4 5 6
```

Filtering and Transforming Tables

1. Filtering

Extract elements from a table that meet a specific condition.

lua

```lua
local numbers = {1, 2, 3, 4, 5, 6}


local function filterEven(tbl)
    local result = {}
    for _, num in ipairs(tbl) do
        if num % 2 == 0 then

table.insert(result, num)
        end
    end
```

```lua
    return result

end


local      evenNumbers      =
filterEven(numbers)


for      _,      num      in
ipairs(evenNumbers) do

    print(num)

end

-- Output: 2 4 6
```

2. Transforming

Apply a function to each element in a table.

lua

```lua
local numbers = {1, 2, 3, 4}

local                   function
squareValues(tbl)
    local result = {}
    for _, num in ipairs(tbl)
do
        table.insert(result,
num * num)
    end
    return result
end
```

```lua
local          squared          =
squareValues(numbers)


for _, num in ipairs(squared)
do

    print(num)

end

-- Output: 1 4 9 16
```

Hands-On Project: Building a Simple To-Do List Application

In this hands-on project, we'll create a simple, console-based To-Do List application using **Lua.** This project will help you apply what you've learned about tables, loops, and functions. By the end, you'll have a functioning tool for managing tasks—a stepping stone to building more complex applications in the future.

Project Overview

The application will allow users to:

1. Add tasks.
2. View all tasks.
3. Mark tasks as completed.
4. Delete tasks.

We'll use **Lua** tables to store the tasks and their statuses.

Step 1: Setting Up the Program

Start by creating a basic structure for the application.

lua

```lua
-- Initialize the tasks table
local tasks = {}


-- Display menu options to the user
local function displayMenu()
    print("\n--- To-Do List Menu ---")

    print("1. Add a new task")

    print("2. View all tasks")

    print("3. Mark a task as completed")
```

```lua
    print("4. Delete a task")

    print("5. Exit")

end
```

Step 2: Adding a Task

We'll create a function to add a task to the tasks table. Each task will have two fields: description and completed.

lua

```lua
-- Function to add a new task

local function addTask()

    print("Enter      the      task
description:")
```

```lua
    local     description     =
io.read()

    table.insert(tasks,
{description  =  description,
completed = false})

    print("Task          added
successfully!")

end
```

Step 3: Viewing All Tasks

To display tasks, iterate through the
tasks table and show each task's status.

lua

```lua
-- Function to view all tasks

local function viewTasks()
```

```lua
    if #tasks == 0 then
        print("No          tasks
found!")
        return
    end


    print("\n--- To-Do List --
-")
    for     i,      task     in
ipairs(tasks) do
    local status = task.completed and
"[✓]" or "[ ]"
        print(i  ..  ".  "  ..
status    ..    "    "    ..
task.description)
    end
```

```
end
```

Step 4: Marking a Task as Completed

This function updates a task's completed status based on the user's choice.

lua

```lua
-- Function to mark a task as
completed

local function completeTask()

    viewTasks()

    print("Enter   the   task
number to mark as completed:")

    local    taskNumber    =
tonumber(io.read())
```

```
    if tasks[taskNumber] then

tasks[taskNumber].completed =
true

        print("Task marked as
completed!")

    else

        print("Invalid    task
number!")

    end

end
```

Step 5: Deleting a Task

Remove a task from the `tasks` table using its index.

lua

```lua
-- Function to delete a task
local function deleteTask()
    viewTasks()
    print("Enter    the    task
number to delete:")
    local    taskNumber    =
tonumber(io.read())


    if tasks[taskNumber] then
        table.remove(tasks,
taskNumber)
```

```lua
        print("Task    deleted
successfully!")
    else
        print("Invalid    task
number!")
    end
end
```

Step 6: Putting It All Together

Combine all the functions into a loop to
create an interactive application.

lua

```lua
-- Main application loop
```

```lua
local function toDoListApp()

    while true do

        displayMenu()

        print("Choose          an
option (1-5):")

        local       choice       =
tonumber(io.read())


        if choice == 1 then

            addTask()

        elseif  choice  ==  2
then

            viewTasks()

        elseif  choice  ==  3
then
```

```lua
            completeTask()

        elseif  choice  ==  4
then

            deleteTask()

        elseif  choice  ==  5
then

            print("Exiting the
application. Goodbye!")

            break

        else

            print("Invalid
option. Please try again.")

        end

    end

end
```

```
-- Start the application

toDoListApp()
```

Key Features

1. **Dynamic Storage:** The tasks are stored in a **Lua** table, making it easy to add, update, and remove items dynamically.
2. **User-Friendly Interface:** The menu-driven interface ensures that users can navigate the application effortlessly.
3. **Extensibility:** This structure can be easily expanded to include

additional features like task prioritization or deadlines.

Sample Output

Menu Display

css

```
--- To-Do List Menu ---

1. Add a new task

2. View all tasks

3. Mark a task as completed

4. Delete a task

5. Exit

Choose an option (1-5):
```

Adding Tasks

arduino

```
Enter the task description:

Buy groceries

Task added successfully!
```

Viewing Tasks

css

```
--- To-Do List ---

1. [ ] Buy groceries

2. [ ] Finish Lua project
```

Marking a Task as Completed

typescript

```
Enter the task number to mark
as completed:

1

Task marked as completed!
```

Deleting Tasks

arduino

```
Enter the task number to
delete:

2

Task deleted successfully!
```

Chapter 4: Advanced Lua Concepts

In this chapter, we dive deeper into **Lua**'s advanced features that give it its reputation as a flexible and lightweight scripting language. You'll learn about coroutines for efficient task management, modules for maintaining organized and reusable code, and file handling for working with external data.

4.1 Coroutines for Parallel Execution

Coroutines are one of **Lua**'s most versatile features, allowing you to handle cooperative multitasking with ease. They differ from threads in that they don't run concurrently. Instead, coroutines enable you to pause and resume execution at specific points, making them ideal for tasks like simulations, game loops, or managing stateful operations.

What Are Coroutines?

A coroutine is a function that can yield control back to its caller and later resume execution from where it left off. This makes coroutines perfect for scenarios where you need to manage multiple tasks without blocking your program.

Key coroutine functions:

1. `coroutine.create(func)`: Creates a coroutine.
2. `coroutine.resume(co)`: Resumes a suspended coroutine.
3. `coroutine.yield()`: Pauses a coroutine.
4. `coroutine.status(co)`: Checks the status of a coroutine

("running", "suspended", or "dead").

5. `coroutine.wrap(func)`: Creates a coroutine and returns it as a function.

Creating and Using Coroutines

Let's break down how to use coroutines step by step.

Creating a Coroutine

To create a coroutine, you wrap a function with `coroutine.create`. The function encapsulates the logic you want to execute in stages.

lua

```
-- A simple coroutine function
```

```lua
local function greet()
    print("Hello")
    coroutine.yield() -- Pause here
    print("Welcome back!")
end


-- Create the coroutine
local          co          =
coroutine.create(greet)


-- Resume the coroutine
coroutine.resume(co)       --
Output: Hello
```

```
coroutine.resume(co)          --
Output: Welcome back!
```

In this example:

- The coroutine starts with
  `coroutine.resume(co)`.
- When it hits
  `coroutine.yield()`, it pauses
  execution.
- Calling
  `coroutine.resume(co)` again
  resumes it from where it paused.

Understanding Coroutine States

Coroutines can have the following states:

- `running`: The coroutine is
  currently executing.

- **suspended**: The coroutine is paused and can be resumed.
- **dead**: The coroutine has finished execution and cannot be resumed.

You can check a coroutine's state with `coroutine.status`.

lua

```lua
local          co          =
coroutine.create(function()

    print("Working...")

end)



print(coroutine.status(co)) --
suspended

coroutine.resume(co)         --
Working...
```

```
print(coroutine.status(co)) --
dead
```

Practical Example: Task Management

Let's use coroutines to manage tasks, such as a simple countdown.

lua

```lua
-- Countdown coroutine
local function countdown(from)
    for i = from, 1, -1 do
        print("Countdown: " ..
i)
```

```lua
        coroutine.yield()    --
Pause execution

    end

    print("Lift-off!")

end


-- Create and use the coroutine

local          co           =
coroutine.create(countdown)

coroutine.resume(co,    5)    --
Countdown: 5

coroutine.resume(co)          --
Countdown: 4

coroutine.resume(co)          --
Countdown: 3
```

This approach gives you precise control over execution, which is particularly useful in game development or real-time applications.

Advanced Coroutine Patterns

Producer-Consumer Model

Coroutines are often used to implement the producer-consumer pattern, where one coroutine produces data and another consumes it.

lua

```lua
-- Producer coroutine
local producer = coroutine.create(function()
    for i = 1, 5 do
```

```lua
        print("Producing: " ..
i)

        coroutine.yield(i)  --
Pass data to the consumer

    end

end)


-- Consumer function

local function consumer()

    while
coroutine.status(producer)  ~=
"dead" do

        local  _,  value  =
coroutine.resume(producer)

        print("Consuming: " ..
value)
```

```
      end

end


-- Start the consumer

consumer()
```

Output:

makefile

```
Producing: 1

Consuming: 1

Producing: 2

Consuming: 2

. . .
```

When to Use Coroutines

Coroutines shine in scenarios like:

1. **Game loops:** Manage events and animations without freezing the program.
2. **Simulations:** Control state changes in systems like particle effects.
3. **Non-blocking I/O:** Manage data streams efficiently.

4.2 Modules and Packages for Modular Code

In **Lua,** modular programming is a cornerstone of writing clean, maintainable, and reusable code. Modules and packages provide a way to organize your code into logical units, making it easier to manage and scale your projects.

What Are Modules?

A module is a **Lua** file that contains a set of functions, variables, and other components designed to be reused in other parts of your program. Modules act as libraries and are loaded using the `require` function.

Creating a Module

To create a module:

1. Write your code in a separate `.lua` file.
2. Return a table that contains the components you want to expose.

Here's a simple example:

lua

```lua
-- math_operations.lua
local math_operations = {}

function
math_operations.add(a, b)

    return a + b

end


function
math_operations.subtract(a, b)

    return a - b

end
```

```
return math_operations
```

This module defines two functions: add
and subtract, encapsulated in a table.

Using a Module

To use a module, save it as a .lua file
and load it in your script with require.

lua

```
-- main.lua

local    math_operations    =
require("math_operations")
```

```lua
local         sum         =
math_operations.add(10, 5)

print("Sum:", sum) -- Output:
Sum: 15


local       difference      =
math_operations.subtract(10,
5)

print("Difference:",
difference)       --      Output:
Difference: 5
```

When using `require`, **Lua** looks for the module in the same directory or specified paths.

Structuring Large Projects with Modules

For larger projects, modules help keep your codebase organized. You can group related functionality into separate files:

css

```
project/

├── main.lua

├── player.lua

├── enemy.lua

└── utilities.lua
```

Each file acts as a module, encapsulating specific logic. For instance:

lua

```
-- player.lua
local player = {}

function player.move()
    print("Player is moving")
end

return player
```

In your main script:

lua

```lua
local        player         =
require("player")

player.move()    --    Output:
Player is moving
```

Packages in Lua

A package is a collection of modules that work together to provide a larger functionality. **Lua** uses the global table package to manage packages.

The package.path variable defines where **Lua** looks for modules. You can extend this path if your modules are in custom directories:

lua

```
package.path = package.path ..
";./modules/?.lua"
```

This adds the `./modules/` directory to the search path.

Creating and Using Packages

Here's how you can organize a package:

csharp

```
math_package/

├── init.lua

├── basic_operations.lua

└── advanced_operations.lua
```

basic_operations.lua:

lua

```lua
local basic_operations = {}

function basic_operations.add(a, b)
    return a + b
end

return basic_operations
```

advanced_operations.lua:

```lua
local advanced_operations = {}

function
advanced_operations.square(a)
    return a * a
end

return advanced_operations
```

init.lua:

The `init.lua` file acts as the entry point for the package.

```lua
```

```lua
local math_package = {}


math_package.basic        =
require("math_package.basic_o
perations")

math_package.advanced     =
require("math_package.advance
d_operations")


return math_package
```

Using the package:

lua

```
local       math_package       =
require("math_package")


print(math_package.basic.add(
10, 5))        -- Output: 15

print(math_package.advanced.s
quare(4))    -- Output: 16
```

Benefits of Modular Code

1. **Reusability:** Write once, use anywhere.
2. **Maintainability:** Changes in one module don't affect the entire codebase.
3. **Collaboration:** Easier to work on large projects as modules encapsulate functionality.

Practical Example: A Utility Module

Let's create a utility module for string manipulation:

lua

```lua
-- string_utils.lua
local string_utils = {}


function string_utils.reverse(str)
    return str:reverse()
end
```

```lua
function
string_utils.is_palindrome(st
r)

    return         str          ==
str:reverse()

end



return string_utils
```

Using the module:

lua

```lua
-- main.lua

local       string_utils       =
require("string_utils")
```

```lua
local word = "level"

print("Reversed:",
string_utils.reverse(word))
-- Output: Reversed: level

print("Is          palindrome?",
string_utils.is_palindrome(wo
rd)) -- Output: Is palindrome?
true
```

4.3 File Handling and External Data Management

File handling is a fundamental aspect of programming, allowing your **Lua** scripts to read from and write to files, as well as manage external data effectively. This capability is essential for building robust applications that interact with user input, save data, or process external datasets.

Basics of File Handling in Lua

Lua provides a set of standard I/O functions for working with files:

- **Opening files:** Using `io.open()`.
- **Reading and writing:** Functions such as `read()` and `write()`.
- **Closing files:** Ensuring resources are properly freed.

Opening and Closing Files

Files in **Lua** can be opened in different modes:

- `"r"`: Read mode (default).

- `"w"`: Write mode (overwrites existing files).
- `"a"`: Append mode.
- `"r+"`: Read and write mode.
- `"w+"`: Read and write mode (overwrites existing files).
- `"a+"`: Read and write mode (appends to file).

Example: Opening and Closing a File

lua

```
local file =
io.open("example.txt", "w") --
Open a file in write mode

if not file then

    print("Error: Unable to
open file.")

    return
```

```lua
end
```

```lua
file:write("Hello, Lua!")  --
Write to the file
```

```lua
file:close() -- Close the file
```

```lua
print("File written and closed
successfully.")
```

Reading from Files

Lua provides multiple ways to read file contents:

1. **Line by Line:** Using `:lines()`.
2. **Whole File:** Using `:read("*a")`.
3. **Fixed Number of Characters:** Using `:read(n)`.

Example: Reading a File Line by Line

lua

```lua
local file = io.open("example.txt", "r") -- Open the file in read mode

if not file then
    print("Error: File not found.")

    return
end


for line in file:lines() do
    print(line)
end
```

```lua
file:close()
```

Example: Reading the Entire File

lua

```lua
local            file            =
io.open("example.txt", "r")
if file then
    local        content        =
file:read("*a")  -- Read  all
content
    print("File Content:\n" ..
content)
    file:close()
else
```

```lua
    print("Error:  Unable   to
open file.")
```

```lua
end
```

Writing to Files

You can write text or data to files using
`:write()`.

Example: Writing Data

lua

```lua
local           file          =
io.open("data.txt", "w")
```

```lua
if file then
```

```lua
    file:write("Line 1: Lua is
powerful!\n")

    file:write("Line 2: File
handling is straightforward.")

    file:close()

    print("Data         written
successfully.")
else

    print("Error: Unable  to
open file for writing.")
end
```

Appending Data

When appending, existing data in the file is preserved, and new data is added to the end.

Example: Appending to a File

lua

```lua
local            file           =
io.open("data.txt", "a")

if file then

    file:write("\nLine        3:
Appending new data.")

    file:close()

    print("Data        appended
successfully.")

else
```

```
    print("Error:   Unable   to
open file for appending.")

end
```

Practical Example: Logging System

Let's create a simple logging system that
appends log messages to a file.

Code Example

lua

```
local                function
log_message(message)
```

```lua
    local          file          =
io.open("log.txt", "a")

    if file then

        local    timestamp    =
os.date("[%Y-%m-%d %H:%M:%S]")

        file:write(timestamp
.. " " .. message .. "\n")

        file:close()

        print("Log          entry
added.")

    else

        print("Error:    Unable
to open log file.")

    end

end
```

```lua
-- Test the logger

log_message("Application
started.")

log_message("User logged in.")
```

External Data Management

Lua can handle external data formats such as JSON, XML, or CSV using additional libraries. For JSON, a commonly used library is **dkjson**.

Working with JSON

1. **Install the library** (if needed).
2. Use it to encode or decode JSON data.

Example: JSON Parsing with dkjson

lua

```lua
local json = require("dkjson")

-- Sample JSON string
local json_string = '{"name":
"John", "age": 30, "skills":
["Lua", "Python"]}'

-- Decode JSON to Lua table
local lua_table, pos, err =
json.decode(json_string)
if err then
    print("Error:", err)
```

```lua
else

    print("Name:",
lua_table.name)

    print("Age:",
lua_table.age)

    print("Skills:",
table.concat(lua_table.skills
, ", "))

end


-- Encode Lua table to JSON

local     encoded_json     =
json.encode(lua_table)

print("Encoded          JSON:",
encoded_json)
```

Best Practices for File Handling

1. **Error Handling**: Always check if the file exists or was opened successfully.
2. **Close Files**: Avoid memory leaks by closing files after use.
3. **Use Libraries**: For complex external data, leverage libraries for easier parsing and manipulation.
4. **Secure Paths**: Avoid hardcoding paths; use relative paths when possible.

4.4 Hands-On Project: Building a File Processing Tool

In this project, we'll develop a simple file processing tool using **Lua**. The tool will read data from a file, process the contents, and output the results to a new file. This type of application is useful for tasks like cleaning data, generating reports, or transforming input formats.

Project Overview

Goal: Create a **Lua** script that:

1. Reads data from an input text file.
2. Processes the data (e.g., converts text to uppercase and counts lines).
3. Outputs the processed data to a new file.
4. Provides feedback to the user about the operation.

Step 1: Setting Up the Environment

Before we begin, ensure you have a text editor and **Lua** installed on your machine. For simplicity, we'll use two files:

- `input.txt`: Contains raw data for processing.
- `output.txt`: Will store the processed data.

Example Content for `input.txt`:

csharp

```
hello world

lua is great for scripting

file processing is useful
```

Step 2: Reading the Input File

First, open the input file and read its contents line by line.

Code Example:

lua

```lua
-- Open the input file in read
mode

local        input_file        =
io.open("input.txt", "r")

if not input_file then

    print("Error:  Unable  to
open input.txt")

    return

end


-- Read all lines into a table
```

```lua
local lines = {}

for line in input_file:lines()
do
    table.insert(lines, line)
end


-- Close the input file
input_file:close()


-- Display the read lines
print("Read      lines      from
input.txt:")
for _, line in ipairs(lines) do
    print(line)
end
```

Step 3: Processing the Data

Let's transform the data by converting each line to uppercase and counting the number of lines.

Code Example:

lua

```
-- Function to convert text to uppercase

local                      function
process_data(lines)

    local processed_lines = {}

    for    _,      line    in
ipairs(lines) do
```

```lua
        table.insert(processed_lines,
string.upper(line))

    end

    return        processed_lines,
#processed_lines  --    Return
processed lines and line count

end



local           processed_lines,
line_count                    =
process_data(lines)

print("\nProcessed lines:")

for       _,        line       in
ipairs(processed_lines) do

    print(line)

end
```

```
print("\nNumber    of    lines
processed:", line_count)
```

Step 4: Writing to the Output File

Next, save the processed data to output.txt.

Code Example:

lua

```lua
-- Open the output file in
write mode

local    output_file    =
io.open("output.txt", "w")
```

```lua
if not output_file then

    print("Error:  Unable   to
open output.txt")

    return

end



-- Write processed lines to the
output file

for        _,        line       in
ipairs(processed_lines) do

    output_file:write(line  ..
"\n")

end



-- Close the output file
```

```
output_file:close()


print("\nProcessed    data    has
been written to output.txt")
```

Step 5: Adding Feedback and Completion Messages

Enhance the tool by adding user-friendly feedback and ensuring robust error handling.

Final Script:

lua

```
-- File Processing Tool
```

```lua
-- Step 1: Read the Input File

local       input_file       =
io.open("input.txt", "r")

if not input_file then

    print("Error:  Unable  to
open  input.txt.  Ensure  the
file exists.")

    return

end


local lines = {}

for line in input_file:lines()
do

    table.insert(lines, line)

end
```

```lua
input_file:close()


print("Successfully read data
from input.txt.")


-- Step 2: Process the Data
local                    function
process_data(lines)

    local processed_lines = {}

    for    _,    line    in
ipairs(lines) do

table.insert(processed_lines,
string.upper(line))

    end
```

```lua
    return    processed_lines,
#processed_lines

end


local          processed_lines,
line_count                    =
process_data(lines)

print(string.format("Processe
d   %d   lines   of   data.",
line_count))


-- Step 3: Write to the Output
File

local      output_file      =
io.open("output.txt", "w")

if not output_file then
```

```lua
        print("Error:  Unable  to
open output.txt for writing.")

        return

end


for          _,         line         in
ipairs(processed_lines) do

        output_file:write(line  ..
"\n")

end

output_file:close()


print("Data        has       been
successfully    written      to
output.txt.")
```

Running the Tool

1. Save the above script as
   `file_processor.lua`.
2. Create an `input.txt` file with
   sample content in the same
   directory.

Run   the   script   using:
bash

```
lua file_processor.lua
```

3.
4. Check `output.txt` for the
   processed data.

Enhancements and Next Steps

This project serves as a foundation for more complex file processing tasks. You could expand it by:

- Adding support for different transformations (e.g., removing whitespace, replacing words).
- Allowing user input for filenames or transformations.
- Handling CSV or JSON files for structured data.

By mastering file handling through practical projects like this, you can confidently build tools that manipulate data efficiently and effectively.

Chapter 5: Object-Oriented Programming in Lua

Object-oriented programming (OOP) is a powerful paradigm that helps developers organize and manage complex codebases. **Lua**, while not natively object-oriented, provides flexible tools for implementing OOP principles such as classes, objects, inheritance, and encapsulation. In this chapter, we'll explore how **Lua** achieves OOP using tables, metatables, and prototypes.

5.1 Implementing Classes and Objects

In **Lua**, the concept of object-oriented programming (OOP) is implemented using tables and metatables. While **Lua** doesn't have built-in OOP syntax like

247

other programming languages, it provides powerful mechanisms to emulate OOP concepts such as classes, objects, inheritance, and encapsulation.

What Are Classes and Objects?

- **Class:** A blueprint for creating objects. It defines properties (attributes) and methods (functions) shared by objects.
- **Object:** An instance of a class, representing a specific entity with its own data.

In **Lua,** both classes and objects are represented as tables.

Creating a Class

Here's how you can define a class in **Lua:**

lua

```lua
-- Define a class as a table
Animal = {}
Animal.__index = Animal  -- Enable method lookups on instances


-- Constructor for the Animal class
function Animal:new(name, sound)
    local instance = setmetatable({}, Animal)  -- Create a new table and set its metatable
```

```lua
    instance.name = name or
"Unnamed Animal"    -- Default
name

    instance.sound = sound or
"Silent"        -- Default sound

    return instance
end


-- Define a method for the
class
function Animal:make_sound()

    print(self.name .. " says:
" .. self.sound)

end
```

Explanation:

1. `Animal.__index = Animal`:
   Sets the `__index` metamethod so that method lookups on an instance refer to the `Animal` table.
2. `setmetatable({}, Animal)`:
   Creates a new object and links it to the `Animal` table.
3. `self`: Refers to the object calling the method.

Creating Objects

To create an object, call the `new` method of the class:

lua

```
-- Create instances of Animal

local cat = Animal:new("Cat",
"Meow")
```

```
local dog = Animal:new("Dog",
"Woof")
```

```
-- Call methods on the objects

cat:make_sound()   --   Output:
Cat says: Meow

dog:make_sound()   --   Output:
Dog says: Woof
```

Adding More Methods

You can extend the functionality of a class by defining more methods:

lua

```lua
function Animal:describe()

    print("This is a " ..
self.name .. ". It says '" ..
self.sound .. "'.")

end



-- Use the new method

cat:describe() -- Output: This
is a Cat. It says 'Meow'.
```

Encapsulation with Private Attributes

Lua does not have a built-in mechanism for private attributes, but you can emulate it using local variables in the constructor.

lua

```lua
function      Animal:new(name,
sound)

    local      instance      =
setmetatable({}, Animal)

    local private_name = name
or "Unnamed Animal" -- Private
attribute

    instance.sound = sound or
"Silent"


    --   Public   methods   to
access private attributes
    function
instance:get_name()

        return private_name
```

```lua
    end


    function
instance:set_name(new_name)
        private_name                =
new_name
    end


    return instance
end


-- Test private attributes
local           bird            =
Animal:new("Bird", "Chirp")
```

```
print(bird:get_name())        --
Output: Bird

bird:set_name("Parrot")

print(bird:get_name())        --
Output: Parrot
```

Benefits of Using Classes

- **Code Reusability:** Define common behavior once and reuse it across objects.
- **Organization:** Keep related data and behavior in one place.
- **Scalability:** Easily extend functionality as projects grow.

Key Concepts in Lua Classes

- **Inheritance:** Allows one class to derive behavior from another (explored in the next section).
- **Polymorphism:** Enables different classes to implement methods with the same name but different behavior.
- **Encapsulation:** Protects object data by controlling access.

Best Practices

1. Use consistent naming conventions for classes and methods.
2. Keep class definitions simple and focused on a single responsibility.
3. Document methods to improve readability and maintainability.

By mastering **Lua**'s class and object implementation, you can create clean, modular, and maintainable codebases that scale with your projects. With tables and metatables as the backbone, **Lua**'s flexibility empowers you to design powerful object-oriented solutions.

5.2 Prototypes and Inheritance Patterns

Inheritance allows one class to reuse the properties and methods of another. **Lua** implements inheritance using metatables.

Creating a Subclass

Let's extend the `Person` class to create a `Student` class.

Code Example:

```
-- Define the Student class

Student = setmetatable({}, Person)

Student.__index = Student


-- Constructor for Student

function Student:new(name, age, major)

    local instance = Person.new(self, name, age) -- Call parent constructor

    instance.major = major or "Undeclared"

    return instance
```

```lua
end


-- Add a method to Student

function Student:display()

    print("Name: " .. self.name .. ", Age: " ..
self.age .. ", Major: " .. self.major)

end


-- Create a Student object

local jane = Student:new("Jane Doe", 22,
"Computer Science")

jane:display()
```

Explanation:

1. `setmetatable({}, Person)`:
   Links the Student class to the
   Person class.
2. `Person.new(self, ...)`: Calls
   the parent constructor to initialize
   common properties.

Overriding Methods

A subclass can override methods from its
parent class by redefining them.

5.3 Structuring Modular and Scalable Code

As projects grow, organizing your code
into modules is crucial for
maintainability.

Using Modules for OOP

You can structure classes into separate files and use `require` to load them.

File: `Person.lua`:

local Person = {}

Person.__index = Person

function Person:new(name, age)

   local instance = setmetatable({}, Person)

   instance.name = name or "Unknown"

   instance.age = age or 0

   return instance

end

```lua
function Person:display()

    print("Name: " .. self.name .. ", Age: " ..
self.age)

end


return Person
```

File: `main.lua`:

```lua
local Person = require("Person")


local john = Person:new("John Doe", 30)

john:display()
```

Explanation:

- **Modules:** Encapsulate logic for reuse and better organization.
- `require`: Loads modules, making them available for use.

5.4 Hands-On Project: Creating a Simple Inventory System

In this hands-on project, you'll build a simple inventory system using **Lua**'s object-oriented programming features and table manipulation techniques. This project will help you understand how to manage collections of items and perform operations such as adding, removing, and displaying items in an organized way.

Project Overview

An inventory system is a core feature in many applications, especially games. This system will include:

1. Adding items to the inventory.
2. Removing items from the inventory.
3. Displaying the current inventory.
4. Searching for a specific item.

Step 1: Define the Inventory Class

We'll use a class-like structure to represent the inventory. This will make it easier to manage and extend the functionality.

Code:

lua

```lua
-- inventory.lua: Inventory
class

local Inventory = {}

Inventory.__index = Inventory


-- Constructor

function Inventory:new()

    local instance = {

        items = {}, -- Table to
store inventory items

    }

    setmetatable(instance,
Inventory)

    return instance
```

```lua
end


-- Add an item to the inventory
function
Inventory:add_item(item_name,
quantity)

    if   self.items[item_name]
then

        self.items[item_name]
=   self.items[item_name]   +
quantity

    else

        self.items[item_name]
= quantity

    end
```

```lua
    print(item_name .. "
added.    Total:    " ..
self.items[item_name])

end


-- Remove an item from the
inventory

function
Inventory:remove_item(item_na
me, quantity)

    if                not
self.items[item_name] then

        print("Error:    " ..
item_name .. " does not exist
in the inventory.")

        return

    end
```

```lua
    if self.items[item_name] <
quantity then

        print("Error:        Not
enough " .. item_name .. " in
the inventory.")

        return

    end

    self.items[item_name]    =
self.items[item_name]          -
quantity

    if   self.items[item_name]
== 0 then

        self.items[item_name]
=  nil  --  Remove  item  if
quantity is zero

    end
```

```lua
    print(item_name    ..    "
removed.    Remaining:    "    ..
(self.items[item_name] or 0))

end


-- Display all items in the
inventory

function
Inventory:display_items()

    print("\nCurrent
Inventory:")

    for item_name, quantity in
pairs(self.items) do

        print("-        "        ..
item_name .. ": " .. quantity)

    end

end
```

```lua
-- Search for an item in the
inventory

function
Inventory:search_item(item_na
me)

    if   self.items[item_name]
then

        print(item_name  ..   "
found.   Quantity:     "     ..
self.items[item_name])

    else

        print(item_name  ..   "
is not in the inventory.")

    end

end
```

```lua
return Inventory
```

Step 2: Main Program

In the main program, we'll create an instance of the inventory and demonstrate how to interact with it.

Code:

lua

```lua
-- main.lua: Using the
Inventory class

local Inventory =
require("inventory")


-- Create a new inventory
```

```lua
local      my_inventory      =
Inventory:new()


-- Add items

my_inventory:add_item("Potion
", 10)

my_inventory:add_item("Sword"
, 1)

my_inventory:add_item("Potion
", 5)


-- Display inventory

my_inventory:display_items()


-- Search for an item
```

```
my_inventory:search_item("Pot
ion")

my_inventory:search_item("Shi
eld")


-- Remove items

my_inventory:remove_item("Pot
ion", 8)

my_inventory:remove_item("Swo
rd", 1)

my_inventory:remove_item("Swo
rd", 1)


-- Display inventory again

my_inventory:display_items()
```

Step 3: Explanation

Adding Items

The `add_item` method checks if the item already exists in the inventory. If it does, it increments the quantity; otherwise, it adds the item.

Removing Items

The `remove_item` method ensures the quantity to be removed is valid and removes the item if the quantity reaches zero.

Displaying Items

The `display_items` method iterates over the `items` table and prints each item and its quantity.

Searching for Items

The `search_item` method checks if an item exists in the inventory and prints its quantity if found.

Step 4: Running the Code

When you run the program, the output will look like this:

yaml

```
Potion added. Total: 10

Sword added. Total: 1

Potion added. Total: 15


Current Inventory:
```

- Potion: 15

- Sword: 1

Potion found. Quantity: 15

Shield is not in the inventory.

Potion removed. Remaining: 7

Sword removed. Remaining: 0

Error: Sword does not exist in the inventory.

Current Inventory:

- Potion: 7

Enhancements to Try

1. **Weight Limits:** Add a maximum weight the inventory can hold.
2. **Item Categories:** Group items by categories (e.g., weapons, consumables).
3. **Serialization:** Save and load the inventory from a file.

Chapter 6: Game Development with Lua

Lua's lightweight nature and simplicity make it an excellent choice for game development, and one of its most popular frameworks, **Love2D**, is an outstanding tool for creating 2D games. In this chapter, we'll explore the basics of using Love2D for game development, covering essential concepts like graphics, input handling, and sound. To bring these ideas together, you'll work on a hands-on project to build a **Pong game** from scratch.

6.1 Introduction to Love2D Framework

Lua is widely used in game development, and its simplicity pairs perfectly with

279

Love2D, an open-source framework designed for 2D game creation. Love2D is lightweight, beginner-friendly, and packed with features, making it an excellent tool for building games. Whether you're creating simple arcade games or more advanced simulations, Love2D provides the tools you need without unnecessary complexity.

Key Features of Love2D

1. **Easy-to-Use API:** Functions for graphics, input, audio, and physics are straightforward and well-documented.
2. **Cross-Platform:** Games made with Love2D run on Windows, macOS, Linux, and mobile platforms.
3. **Community Support:** A robust community and a wealth of

resources help you learn and troubleshoot effectively.

Installing Love2D

Getting started with Love2D is simple. Follow these steps:

Step 1: Download Love2D

Visit the official Love2D website and download the version compatible with your operating system.

Step 2: Install Love2D

Run the downloaded installer and follow the instructions. Once installed, you can run Love2D from the command line or by dragging your game folder onto the Love2D executable.

Step 3: Set Up Your First Project

1. Create a new folder for your game, e.g., `MyFirstGame`.
2. Inside the folder, create a file named `main.lua`. This file serves as the entry point for your game.

Step 4: Running Your Game

To test your game:

- **Windows/macOS**: Drag the project folder onto the Love2D executable.

Command Line: Use the following command:
sh

```
love MyFirstGame
```

-

Understanding Love2D's Structure

Love2D organizes game code using three main functions:

1. `love.load`: Executes once when the game starts. Use it to initialize variables and load assets.
2. `love.update`: Runs continuously to handle game logic and updates. It receives a `dt` (delta time) parameter to ensure smooth behavior across different frame rates.
3. `love.draw`: Handles rendering by drawing shapes, images, and text on the screen.

Basic Example:

Here's a simple Love2D program:

lua

```lua
function love.load()

    -- Initialize variables

    x = 100

    y = 100

    speed = 200

end


function love.update(dt)

    -- Move the square to the
right

    x = x + speed * dt

end
```

```
function love.draw()

    -- Draw a blue rectangle

    love.graphics.setColor(0,
0, 1) -- RGB color: Blue


love.graphics.rectangle("fill
", x, y, 50, 50)

end
```

- **love.load** sets up the initial position and speed of the rectangle.
- **love.update** updates the position of the rectangle based on the frame time.
- **love.draw** renders the rectangle on the screen.

Core Love2D Modules

1. Graphics (`love.graphics`)

The graphics module is used to draw shapes, images, and text.

Example: Drawing Shapes

lua

```
function love.draw()

    love.graphics.setColor(1,
0, 0) -- Red


love.graphics.circle("fill",
200, 150, 50) -- Draw a filled
circle
```

```lua
    love.graphics.setColor(0,
1, 0) -- Green

love.graphics.rectangle("line
", 50, 50, 100, 100) -- Draw an
outlined rectangle

end
```

2. Input Handling (`love.keyboard`)

Love2D captures user input, such as key presses.

Example: Detecting Key Presses

lua

```lua
function love.keypressed(key)
    if key == "space" then
```

```lua
        print("Spacebar
pressed!")

    elseif key == "escape"
then

        love.event.quit()    --
Exit the game

    end

end
```

3. Sound (`love.audio`)

Play sound effects and music using the audio module.

Example: Playing a Sound

lua

```lua
local sound
```

```lua
function love.load()

    sound                      =
love.audio.newSource("jump.wa
v", "static")

end


function love.keypressed(key)

    if key == "j" then

        sound:play()  --  Play
sound on 'j' key press

    end

end
```

4. Physics (`love.physics`)

For games involving realistic interactions, the physics module offers built-in support for simulations.

Example: Setting Up a Physics World

lua

```
local world, ground


function love.load()
    love.physics.setMeter(64)
-- 1 meter = 64 pixels

    world                      =
love.physics.newWorld(0,  9.81
* 64, true) -- Gravity
```

```lua
    -- Create ground

    ground = {}

    ground.body              =
love.physics.newBody(world,
400, 550, "static")

    ground.shape             =
love.physics.newRectangleShap
e(800, 20)

    ground.fixture           =
love.physics.newFixture(groun
d.body, ground.shape)

end


function love.update(dt)

    world:update(dt) -- Update
physics world
```

```
end

function love.draw()

love.graphics.setColor(0.3,
0.3, 0.3)

love.graphics.polygon("fill",
ground.body:getWorldPoints(gr
ound.shape:getPoints()))

end
```

Getting Help and Resources

- **Official Documentation:** The
  Love2D wiki is a comprehensive
  resource.

- **Community Forums:** Engage with other developers on the Love2D forums.
- **Open-Source Games:** Study existing projects on platforms like GitHub.

6.2 Creating 2D Games: Graphics, Input, and Sound

2D game development is an exciting way to unleash creativity, and Love2D makes it straightforward with its powerful modules for graphics, input, and sound. In this chapter, we'll explore how to create engaging 2D games using Love2D, covering essential features such as rendering visuals, handling player input, and adding immersive sound effects.

Graphics in Love2D

The `love.graphics` module is at the heart of rendering visuals in Love2D. It allows you to draw shapes, images, and text to bring your game to life.

Drawing Basic Shapes

Love2D supports rendering primitive shapes such as rectangles, circles, and polygons.

lua

```lua
function love.draw()
    -- Set color to red
    love.graphics.setColor(1,
0, 0)

    -- Draw a filled rectangle
```

```
love.graphics.rectangle("fill
", 100, 100, 200, 150)


    -- Set color to blue

    love.graphics.setColor(0,
0, 1)

    -- Draw a filled circle


love.graphics.circle("fill",
300, 300, 50)

end
```

- **setColor**: Defines the drawing
  color in RGB format (values range
  from 0 to 1).

- **`rectangle`**: Draws a rectangle (mode: `"fill"` for filled, `"line"` for outline).
- **`circle`**: Draws a circle with specified radius and position.

Working with Images

To include visuals like sprites or backgrounds, use the `love.graphics.newImage` function.

lua

```
local background
```

```
function love.load()
    -- Load an image
```

```lua
    background                =
love.graphics.newImage("backg
round.png")

end


function love.draw()

    -- Draw the image at the
top-left corner


love.graphics.draw(background
, 0, 0)

end
```

Pro Tip: Always ensure images are in the project directory to avoid loading issues.

Handling Input

Interactive games require capturing player input. Love2D supports keyboard, mouse, and gamepad inputs through its `love.keyboard`, `love.mouse`, and `love.joystick` modules.

Keyboard Input

The `love.keypressed` and `love.keyreleased` functions detect when a key is pressed or released.

lua

```lua
local message = "Press any key!"



function love.keypressed(key)
```

```
    message = "You pressed: "
.. key

end


function love.keyreleased(key)

    message = "You released: "
.. key

end


function love.draw()


love.graphics.print(message,
200, 200) -- Display the
message

end
```

Mouse Input

Capture mouse clicks or movement using `love.mousepressed` and `love.mousereleased`.

lua

```lua
local mouseX, mouseY


function love.mousepressed(x, y, button)
    mouseX, mouseY = x, y
end


function love.draw()
    if mouseX and mouseY then
```

```
love.graphics.setColor(0,    1,
0)


love.graphics.circle("fill",
mouseX, mouseY, 10) -- Draw a
dot at click location

    end

end
```

- **x, y**: The mouse coordinates where the event occurred.
- **button**: Indicates which mouse button was clicked.

Adding Sound Effects and Music

Sound enhances the gaming experience by creating atmosphere and feedback for player actions. Love2D's `love.audio` module manages sound effects and music.

Playing Sound Effects

Sound effects are small audio files triggered during gameplay, such as when a player scores or collects an item.

lua

```
local jumpSound


function love.load()
    -- Load a sound file
```

```
    jumpSound                    =
love.audio.newSource("jump.wa
v", "static")

end



function love.keypressed(key)

    if key == "space" then

        jumpSound:play()      --
Play sound when the spacebar is
pressed

    end

end
```

Looping Background Music

Looping music plays continuously in the
background to set the game's mood.

```lua
local backgroundMusic

function love.load()
    -- Load music and set it to
loop
    backgroundMusic        =
love.audio.newSource("backgro
und.mp3", "stream")

backgroundMusic:setLooping(tr
ue)
    backgroundMusic:play()
end
```

Integrating Graphics, Input, and Sound

Let's combine these concepts into a simple interactive game: a player controls a character using the keyboard while collecting items to earn points.

Code Example: Simple Interactive Game

lua

```lua
local player = {x = 200, y = 200, speed = 150}

local items = {}

local score = 0

local pickupSound


function love.load()
```

```lua
    -- Generate items at
random positions

    for i = 1, 5 do

        table.insert(items, {x
= math.random(50, 750), y =
math.random(50, 550)})

    end



    -- Load pickup sound

    pickupSound              =
love.audio.newSource("pickup.
wav", "static")

end


function love.update(dt)
```

```lua
    -- Move player based on
arrow keys
    if
love.keyboard.isDown("up")
then
        player.y = player.y -
player.speed * dt
    end
    if
love.keyboard.isDown("down")
then
        player.y = player.y +
player.speed * dt
    end
    if
love.keyboard.isDown("left")
then
```

```lua
        player.x = player.x -
player.speed * dt

    end

    if
love.keyboard.isDown("right")
then

        player.x = player.x +
player.speed * dt

    end


    --    Check    for    item
collection

    for i = #items, 1, -1 do

        local item = items[i]

        if math.abs(player.x -
item.x)      <      20      and
```

```lua
math.abs(player.y - item.y) <
20 then

table.remove(items, i)

            score = score + 1

pickupSound:play()    --    Play
pickup sound

        end

    end

end


function love.draw()

    -- Draw player

    love.graphics.setColor(0,
1, 0) -- Green
```

```lua
    love.graphics.rectangle("fill
", player.x, player.y, 30, 30)


    -- Draw items

    love.graphics.setColor(1,
0, 0) -- Red

    for     _,    item    in
ipairs(items) do

love.graphics.circle("fill",
item.x, item.y, 10)

    end


    -- Display score

    love.graphics.setColor(1,
1, 1) -- White
```

```
love.graphics.print("Score:    "
.. score, 10, 10)

end
```

6.3 Hands-On Project: Building a Pong Game with Love2D

Pong is one of the simplest and most iconic video games. It's an excellent starting point to understand 2D game development, as it combines core concepts like handling user input, collisions, and game logic. In this project, we'll build a fully functional Pong game using Love2D.

Step 1: Setting Up the Game

Define the Game Window

We'll set up the game window in `love.conf`.

lua

```
function love.conf(t)
    t.window.title = "Pong Game"
    t.window.width = 800
    t.window.height = 600
end
```

- **t.window.title**: Sets the window title.

- `t.window.width` &
  `t.window.height`: Defines the
  dimensions of the game window.

Initialize Variables

Create a new file, `main.lua`, and
initialize the key variables for paddles,
ball, and scores.

lua

```
-- Window dimensions

local           windowWidth,
windowHeight = 800, 600


-- Paddle properties

local           paddleWidth,
paddleHeight = 20, 100
```

```lua
local paddleSpeed = 300


-- Ball properties

local ballSize = 20

local ballSpeed = 300


-- Positions

local player1 = {x = 30, y =
windowHeight      /      2      -
paddleHeight / 2, score = 0}

local    player2    =    {x    =
windowWidth    -    50,    y    =
windowHeight      /      2      -
paddleHeight / 2, score = 0}

local ball = {x = windowWidth
/  2  -  ballSize  /  2,  y  =
windowHeight / 2 - ballSize /
```

```
2, dx = ballSpeed, dy =
ballSpeed}
```

Step 2: Drawing the Game

In the `love.draw` function, render the paddles, ball, and scores.

lua

```lua
function love.draw()
    -- Background color
    love.graphics.clear(0.1,
0.1, 0.1) -- Dark gray


    -- Draw paddles
```

```
    love.graphics.setColor(1,
1, 1) -- White


love.graphics.rectangle("fill
",    player1.x,    player1.y,
paddleWidth, paddleHeight)


love.graphics.rectangle("fill
",    player2.x,    player2.y,
paddleWidth, paddleHeight)


    -- Draw ball


love.graphics.rectangle("fill
",  ball.x,  ball.y,  ballSize,
ballSize)


    -- Draw scores
```

```lua
    love.graphics.print("Player 1:
" .. player1.score, 50, 10)


    love.graphics.print("Player 2:
"            ..            player2.score,
windowWidth - 150, 10)

end
```

Step 3: Adding Movement

Paddle Movement

Use the `love.update` function to move
the paddles based on keyboard input.

lua

```lua
function love.update(dt)

    -- Player 1 controls (W and
S keys)

    if
love.keyboard.isDown("w") then

        player1.y          =
math.max(0,    player1.y    -
paddleSpeed * dt)

    elseif
love.keyboard.isDown("s") then

        player1.y          =
math.min(windowHeight       -
paddleHeight,   player1.y   +
paddleSpeed * dt)

    end
```

```lua
    -- Player 2 controls (Up
and Down arrow keys)
    if
love.keyboard.isDown("up")
then
        player2.y        =
math.max(0,      player2.y    -
paddleSpeed * dt)

    elseif
love.keyboard.isDown("down")
then
        player2.y        =
math.min(windowHeight        -
paddleHeight,    player2.y    +
paddleSpeed * dt)

    end
end
```

Ball Movement

Update the ball's position and implement basic boundary collision.

lua

```lua
function love.update(dt)
    -- Ball movement

    ball.x = ball.x + ball.dx * dt

    ball.y = ball.y + ball.dy * dt


    -- Ball collision with top and bottom walls

    if ball.y <= 0 or ball.y + ballSize >= windowHeight then
```

```lua
        ball.dy = -ball.dy --
Reverse direction

    end

end
```

Step 4: Collision Detection

Detect and handle collisions between the
ball and paddles.

lua

```lua
function    checkCollision(ax,
ay, aw, ah, bx, by, bw, bh)

    return ax < bx + bw and ax
+ aw > bx and ay < by + bh and
ay + ah > by
```

```lua
end


function love.update(dt)
    -- Ball collision with
paddles

    if checkCollision(ball.x,
ball.y, ballSize, ballSize,
player1.x,          player1.y,
paddleWidth,     paddleHeight)
then

        ball.dx = -ball.dx

    elseif
checkCollision(ball.x, ball.y,
ballSize, ballSize, player2.x,
player2.y,         paddleWidth,
paddleHeight) then

        ball.dx = -ball.dx
```

```lua
        end

end
```

Step 5: Scoring System

Award points when the ball passes a paddle.

lua

```lua
function love.update(dt)

    -- Ball out of bounds

    if ball.x < 0 then

        player2.score        =
player2.score + 1

        resetBall()
```

```
    elseif        ball.x        >
windowWidth then

        player1.score        =
player1.score + 1

        resetBall()

    end

end


function resetBall()

    ball.x = windowWidth / 2 -
ballSize / 2

    ball.y = windowHeight / 2
- ballSize / 2

    ball.dx = -ball.dx

end
```

Step 6: Polishing the Game

Add finishing touches like game restart and improving the ball speed over time.

lua

```lua
function love.keypressed(key)

    if key == "r" then

        -- Reset game

        player1.score = 0

        player2.score = 0

        resetBall()

    end
```

```lua
end


function love.update(dt)

    -- Increase ball speed

    ball.dx    =    ball.dx    +
(ball.dx > 0 and 10 or -10) *
dt

    ball.dy    =    ball.dy    +
(ball.dy > 0 and 10 or -10) *
dt

end
```

Complete Code

Here's the full code for reference:

lua

```lua
-- Pong Game with Love2D

local windowWidth,
windowHeight = 800, 600

local paddleWidth,
paddleHeight = 20, 100

local paddleSpeed = 300

local ballSize = 20

local ballSpeed = 300


local player1 = {x = 30, y =
250, score = 0}
```

```lua
local player2 = {x = 750, y =
250, score = 0}

local ball = {x = 390, y = 290,
dx = ballSpeed, dy = ballSpeed}



function love.load()


love.window.setMode(windowWid
th, windowHeight)


love.window.setTitle("Pong
Game")

end



function love.update(dt)

    -- Paddle movement
```

```lua
    if
love.keyboard.isDown("w") then
player1.y    =    math.max(0,
player1.y - paddleSpeed * dt)
end

    if
love.keyboard.isDown("s") then
player1.y                     =
math.min(windowHeight       -
paddleHeight,    player1.y    +
paddleSpeed * dt) end

    if
love.keyboard.isDown("up")
then  player2.y = math.max(0,
player2.y - paddleSpeed * dt)
end

    if
love.keyboard.isDown("down")
then          player2.y        =
math.min(windowHeight       -
```

```lua
paddleHeight,    player2.y    +
paddleSpeed * dt) end



    -- Ball movement

    ball.x = ball.x + ball.dx
* dt

    ball.y = ball.y + ball.dy
* dt



    -- Ball collision

    if ball.y <= 0 or ball.y +
ballSize >= windowHeight then
ball.dy = -ball.dy end

    if  checkCollision(ball.x,
ball.y,   ballSize,   ballSize,
player1.x,             player1.y,
paddleWidth, paddleHeight) or
```

```lua
    checkCollision(ball.x,
ball.y,  ballSize,  ballSize,
player2.x,        player2.y,
paddleWidth,     paddleHeight)
then

        ball.dx = -ball.dx

    end


    -- Scoring

    if   ball.x  <  0   then
player2.score = player2.score
+ 1; resetBall() end

    if  ball.x  >  windowWidth
then      player1.score    =
player1.score + 1; resetBall()
end

end
```

```
function love.draw()

    love.graphics.clear(0.1,
0.1, 0.1)

    love.graphics.setColor(1,
1, 1)


love.graphics.rectangle("fill
",    player1.x,    player1.y,
paddleWidth, paddleHeight)


love.graphics.rectangle("fill
",    player2.x,    player2.y,
paddleWidth, paddleHeight)


love.graphics.rectangle("fill
",  ball.x,  ball.y,  ballSize,
ballSize)
```

```lua
    love.graphics.print("Player 1:
" .. player1.score, 50, 10)


    love.graphics.print("Player 2:
"           ..           player2.score,
windowWidth - 150, 10)

end



function    checkCollision(ax,
ay, aw, ah, bx, by, bw, bh)

    return ax < bx + bw and ax
+ aw > bx and ay < by + bh and
ay + ah > by

end



function resetBall()
```

```
    ball.x = 390

    ball.y = 290

    ball.dx = -ball.dx

end
```

This Pong game covers essential game development concepts: rendering, input handling, collision detection, and scoring. You can expand on this project by adding power-ups, difficulty

Chapter 7: Lua for Scripting and Automation

Lua's lightweight nature and flexibility make it an excellent choice for scripting and automation tasks. In this chapter, we will explore how **Lua** can automate repetitive tasks, manipulate data, and streamline workflows. By the end, you'll have a practical understanding of using **Lua** for scripting and automation, capped off with a hands-on project.

7.1 Writing Scripts for Task Automation

Scripting repetitive or time-consuming tasks is one of **Lua**'s most practical applications. Its simplicity and flexibility make it an excellent choice for automating workflows, managing files, and even scheduling system operations. This section covers key concepts and examples to help you write powerful automation scripts.

Understanding Task Automation

Task automation involves writing scripts that execute predefined actions without manual intervention. For example, you might automate:

1. File renaming.
2. Data backups.
3. Running system commands.
4. Data parsing and logging.

Lua excels in these scenarios because of its lightweight syntax and comprehensive libraries like **os, io,** and third-party tools such as **LuaFileSystem** (lfs).

Automating File Management

File management is a common automation task. Let's start with an example of organizing files into folders based on their extensions.

Organizing Files by Extension

lua

```lua
-- Import LuaFileSystem (lfs)
local lfs = require("lfs")


-- Define source and target directories
local sourceDir = "./unsorted_files/"
```

```lua
local        targetDir        =
"./organized_files/"


-- Create a folder for a
specific extension

local                function
createFolder(ext)

    local    folderPath    =
targetDir .. ext

    if                    not
lfs.attributes(folderPath,
"mode") then

        lfs.mkdir(folderPath)
-- Create the folder if it
doesn't exist

    end

    return folderPath
```

```lua
end


-- Organize files based on
extensions

local function organizeFiles()
    for        file        in
lfs.dir(sourceDir) do

        if file ~= "." and file
~= ".." then

            local    ext    =
file:match("%.([a-zA-Z0-
9]+)$")    --    Extract    the
extension

            if ext then

                local
folderPath = createFolder(ext)
```

```lua
            os.rename(sourceDir .. file,
folderPath .. "/" .. file)

                print("Moved:
" .. file .. " -> " ..
folderPath)

            end

        end

    end

end


-- Execute the script

organizeFiles()
```

- **lfs.attributes**: Checks if a
  folder already exists.

- `os.rename`: Moves files to their respective folders.
- `file:match`: Captures the file extension.

Automating Repeated Tasks

Scheduling Daily Backups

Automation can save time by performing daily backups without human intervention. Here's a **Lua** script for creating timestamped backups of a directory.

lua

```
-- Backup script
```

```lua
local        sourceDir        =
"./important_files/"

local backupDir = "./backups/"


-- Function to create a
timestamped folder

local              function
createBackupFolder()

    local    timestamp    =
os.date("%Y-%m-%d_%H-%M-%S")

    local    folderPath    =
backupDir  ..  "backup_"  ..
timestamp

    os.execute("mkdir -p " ..
folderPath)

    return folderPath
end
```

```lua
-- Function to copy files
local function copyFiles(src,
dest)
    os.execute("cp -r " .. src
.. "* " .. dest)
end


-- Perform the backup
local function performBackup()
    local    backupFolder    =
createBackupFolder()
    copyFiles(sourceDir,
backupFolder)
    print("Backup completed: "
.. backupFolder)
```

```
end


-- Run the script

performBackup()
```

- **os.date**: Generates a timestamp for unique folder names.
- **os.execute**: Runs shell commands like creating directories or copying files.

Automating System Commands

Lua's os library can run shell commands directly, making it ideal for system-level scripting.

Monitoring Disk Usage

This script monitors disk usage and alerts if usage exceeds a threshold.

lua

```
-- Disk usage monitoring

local threshold = 80 --
Percentage threshold for disk
usage

local function
checkDiskUsage()
```

```lua
    local         handle         =
io.popen("df -h | grep '/$' |
awk '{print $5}'")

    local         result         =
handle:read("*a")

    handle:close()



    local         usage          =
tonumber(result:match("(%d+)"
))

    if   usage   and   usage   >
threshold then

        print("Warning:   Disk
usage is at " .. usage .. "%!")

    else
```

```lua
        print("Disk  usage  is
at  "  ..  usage  ..  "%,  within
safe limits.")

    end

end


-- Execute the function

checkDiskUsage()
```

- **io.popen**: Executes a shell command and captures its output.
- **tonumber**: Converts string output into a numeric value.

Enhancing Productivity with Scripts

Automating Daily Email Reports

Lua can interface with external programs to send automated emails, for example, using **curl.**

lua

```
-- Send an automated email



local                   function
sendEmail(subject,          body,
recipient)

    local      command       =
string.format(

        'curl      -s      --url
"smtps://smtp.example.com:465
" --user "username:password" '
    ..
```

```lua
        '--mail-from
"you@example.com"  --mail-rcpt
"%s" ' ..

        '--upload-file  <(echo
"Subject: %s\n\n%s")',

        recipient,     subject,
body
    )

    os.execute(command)

    print("Email sent to " ..
recipient)
end


-- Usage
sendEmail(
    "Daily Report",
```

```
    "Hello,\n\nThis    is    your
automated              daily
report.\n\nRegards,\nYour  Lua
Script",

    "recipient@example.com"

)
```

- **curl**: Command-line tool to send emails via SMTP.
- **string.format**: Formats strings with dynamic content.

Best Practices for Writing Automation Scripts

1. **Error Handling**:
   ○ Anticipate errors, such as missing files or incorrect permissions.

- Use `pcall` to handle potential runtime issues gracefully.

2. **Modularity:**
   - Break your script into reusable functions for better organization.

3. **Logging:**
   - Maintain logs of automated actions for debugging and auditing.

4. **Environment Testing:**
   - Test scripts in a controlled environment before deploying them.

7.2 Parsing Data and File Manipulation

Parsing data and manipulating files are essential skills for many programming tasks, from handling configuration files to processing large datasets. **Lua's** lightweight and efficient design, combined with its rich set of libraries, makes it an excellent choice for these operations.

Introduction to Data Parsing

Data parsing involves converting structured or semi-structured data into a format suitable for manipulation or analysis. Common formats include:

1. **Text Files:** Line-based or delimited by specific characters (e.g., CSV, TSV).
2. **JSON:** A popular format for structured data exchange.
3. **XML:** Often used in legacy systems or specific APIs.

Reading and Writing Files in Lua

Lua provides straightforward functions for file operations through its **io** library.

Reading Files

Here's an example of reading a file line-by-line:

lua

```
-- Open the file in read mode
local           file         =
io.open("data.txt", "r")



-- Check if the file exists
if not file then
```

```lua
        print("File not found!")
        return
end


-- Read and print each line
for line in file:lines() do
        print(line)
end


-- Close the file
file:close()
```

- **io.open**: Opens the file in the specified mode (" r " for read).

- **`file:lines`**: Iterates through each line in the file.

Writing to Files

You can write data to a file using the `"w"` mode:

lua

```
-- Open the file in write mode
local           file           =
io.open("output.txt", "w")


-- Write some data
file:write("Hello, Lua!\n")
file:write("This   is   a   file
manipulation example.\n")
```

```
-- Close the file

file:close()


print("Data       written       to
output.txt.")
```

Parsing Delimited Text Files (e.g., CSV)

Delimited text files, such as CSV, are widely used for storing tabular data. Let's parse a CSV file and extract its contents.

Example: Parsing a CSV File

Suppose you have a file `data.csv`:

graphql

```
Name,Age,Email

Alice,30,alice@example.com

Bob,25,bob@example.com

Charlie,35,charlie@example.co
m
```

Here's a **Lua** script to parse this file:

lua

```lua
-- Function to split a string
by a delimiter

local    function    split(str,
delimiter)

    local result = {}
```

```lua
    for match in (str ..
delimiter):gmatch("(.-)" ..
delimiter) do

        table.insert(result,
match)

    end

    return result

end



-- Open the CSV file

local        file        =
io.open("data.csv", "r")



-- Check if the file exists

if not file then
```

```lua
    print("CSV     file     not
found!")

    return

end


-- Read and parse the file

local headers = nil

for line in file:lines() do

    if not headers then

        --    The    first    line
contains headers

        headers = split(line,
",")

    else

        -- Parse the data rows
```

```lua
        local     values    =
split(line, ",")

        for    i,    header    in
ipairs(headers) do

            print(header .. ":
" .. values[i])

        end

        print("---")

    end

end


-- Close the file

file:close()
```

- **split**: A utility function to break a string into parts based on a delimiter.
- **Dynamic Parsing**: The script dynamically matches values to their corresponding headers.

Working with JSON

JSON is a widely used format for data exchange. **Lua** supports JSON parsing through libraries like **dkjson** or **cjson**.

Example: Parsing JSON Data

Install **dkjson** and use it as follows:

lua

```lua
-- Import the dkjson library
local json = require("dkjson")
```

```lua
-- Example JSON string
local jsonString = [[
{
    "name": "Alice",
    "age": 30,
    "skills":          ["Lua",
"Python", "JavaScript"]
}
]]


-- Decode JSON to a Lua table
local    data,    _,    err    =
json.decode(jsonString)
if err then
```

```lua
    print("Error     decoding
JSON:", err)

    return

end


-- Access and print the data

print("Name:", data.name)

print("Age:", data.age)

print("Skills:")

for    _,    skill    in
ipairs(data.skills) do

    print("-", skill)

end
```

- **json.decode**: Converts a JSON string into a **Lua** table.
- **Table Access:** Data is accessed using **Lua**'s table syntax.

Writing JSON Data

You can also encode **Lua** tables into JSON:

lua

```
-- Encode Lua table into JSON
local luaTable = {

    name = "Bob",

    age = 25,

    skills = {"Lua", "Go",
"Rust"}

}
```

```
local          jsonString          =
json.encode(luaTable,    {indent
= true})

print(jsonString)
```

- **json.encode**: Converts **Lua**
  tables into JSON strings.
- **{indent = true}**: Adds
  indentation for better readability.

Manipulating Data

Once the data is parsed, you can
manipulate it using **Lua**'s table functions.

Example: Filtering Data

Let's filter rows where age is greater than
30 from a CSV file:

lua

```lua
local                 function
filterData(csvFile)
    local       file        =
io.open(csvFile, "r")
    if not file then return {}
end


    local headers = nil
    local filteredRows = {}


    for line in file:lines()
do
```

```lua
    if not headers then

        headers            =
split(line, ",")

    else

        local    values   =
split(line, ",")

        local      age      =
tonumber(values[2])          --
Assuming 'Age' is the second
column

        if age > 30 then


table.insert(filteredRows,
values)

        end

    end

end
```

```lua
    file:close()

    return filteredRows

end


local          rows         =
filterData("data.csv")

for _, row in ipairs(rows) do

    print("Name:",       row[1],
"Age:", row[2])

end
```

Tips for Effective File Manipulation

1. **Close Files:** Always close files to
   avoid resource leaks.

2. **Error Handling:** Check for errors while opening files or decoding data.

3. **Validation:** Validate data before processing to prevent runtime issues.

4. **Utility Functions:** Create reusable functions for tasks like splitting strings or encoding JSON.

7.3 Real-World Automation Projects

Automation saves time and reduces repetitive tasks, making it a powerful application of **Lua.** By automating workflows, you can improve efficiency and ensure consistency across projects. This section will explore real-world automation scenarios you can tackle using **Lua.**

Why Lua for Automation?

Lua's lightweight nature and ease of integration make it ideal for scripting in various environments, from standalone systems to embedded applications. Its compatibility with libraries and external tools allows developers to build robust automation solutions quickly.

Real-World Scenarios

1. Log File Analysis

Automating log file parsing can help extract insights and detect anomalies in systems or applications.

Example: Filtering Errors from a Log File

lua

```lua
-- Function to filter lines
containing a specific keyword
local                function
filterLogs(logFile, keyword)
    local       file      =
io.open(logFile, "r")
    if not file then
        print("Log  file  not
found!")
        return
    end

    local results = {}
    for line in file:lines()
do
```

```lua
        if  line:find(keyword) then

table.insert(results, line)

        end

    end


    file:close()


    return results

end


-- Example usage
```

```lua
local       errorLogs        =
filterLogs("system.log",
"ERROR")

if #errorLogs > 0 then

    print("Found error logs:")

    for      _,     log      in
ipairs(errorLogs) do

        print(log)

    end

else

    print("No     error     logs
found.")

end
```

This script scans a log file for lines containing the keyword "ERROR" and extracts them.

---

2. Batch File Renaming

Renaming multiple files in a directory is a tedious task when done manually. **Lua** can automate it efficiently.

Example: Renaming Files to Add a Prefix

lua

```
-- Function to rename files in
a directory

local lfs = require("lfs") --
LuaFileSystem library
```

```lua
local                    function
renameFiles(directory, prefix)

    for            file            in
lfs.dir(directory) do

        if file ~= "." and file
~= ".." then

            local   oldPath   =
directory .. "/" .. file

            local   newPath   =
directory .. "/" .. prefix ..
file


os.rename(oldPath, newPath)

        end

    end

    print("Files         renamed
successfully!")
```

```
end
```

```
-- Example usage
renameFiles("my_folder",
"new_")
```

This script adds a specified prefix (e.g., "new_") to all files in a directory.

---

3. Automated Data Processing

Automating tasks like data transformation or aggregation can streamline workflows.

Example: Aggregating Data from Multiple CSV Files

lua

```lua
local                     function
aggregateCSV(inputDir,
outputFile)

    local        output        =
io.open(outputFile, "w")

    if not output then

        print("Could        not
create output file.")

        return

    end



    for          file         in
lfs.dir(inputDir) do

        if
file:match("%.csv$") then
```

```lua
        local   input   =
io.open(inputDir  ..  "/"  ..
file, "r")

        if input then

            for   line   in
input:lines() do

output:write(line .. "\n")
            end

            input:close()
        end
    end

    output:close()
```

```lua
    print("Data       aggregated
into " .. outputFile)

end


-- Example usage

aggregateCSV("data_folder",
"aggregated_data.csv")
```

This script consolidates all CSV files in a directory into a single file.

---

4. API Integration and Automation

Lua can interact with REST APIs to fetch data or trigger events.

Example: Fetching Weather Data

Using a **Lua** HTTP library like **luasocket** or **http,** you can automate API requests:

lua

```lua
local http = require("socket.http")

local json = require("dkjson")


local function fetchWeather(city)

    local apiKey = "your_api_key"

    local url = "http://api.openweathermap.org/data/2.5/weather?q=" .. city .. "&appid=" .. apiKey
```

```lua
    local response, status =
http.request(url)

    if status == 200 then

        local weatherData =
json.decode(response)

        print("Weather in " ..
city .. ": " ..
weatherData.weather[1].descri
ption)

    else

        print("Failed to fetch
weather data.")

    end

end
```

```
-- Example usage

fetchWeather("London")
```

This script retrieves and displays the current weather for a given city using an API.

---

5. Task Scheduling

Lua scripts can schedule and execute tasks based on time or events.

Example: Automated Backups

lua

```
local                    function
backupFile(source,
destination)
```

```lua
    local    sourceFile    =
io.open(source, "r")

    if not sourceFile then

        print("Source file not
found!")

        return

    end


    local    destFile    =
io.open(destination, "w")


destFile:write(sourceFile:rea
d("*all"))


    sourceFile:close()

    destFile:close()
```

```lua
    print("Backup completed: "
.. destination)

end



-- Example usage: Schedule
this with an external tool like
cron

backupFile("important_data.tx
t",    "backup/important_data_"
..    os.date("%Y%m%d")    ..
".txt")
```

This script backs up a file, appending the current date to its name for versioning.

Tools and Libraries to Enhance Automation

- **LuaSocket:** Enables networking capabilities for tasks like HTTP requests and FTP transfers.
- **LuaFileSystem (lfs):** Facilitates file and directory operations.
- **Penlight:** Offers utility functions for string manipulation, file handling, and table operations.

Tips for Real-World Automation

1. **Error Handling:** Always handle errors gracefully, especially for file I/O or network operations.
2. **Scalability:** Use modular scripts that can be reused or extended.
3. **Documentation:** Comment your scripts for clarity and maintainability.

4. **Testing:** Test scripts thoroughly in a controlled environment before deploying.

Hands-On Project: Automating File Sorting Tasks

File sorting is a common task that can quickly become tedious when done manually. Automating this process not only saves time but also ensures consistency and efficiency. In this hands-on project, we will use **Lua** to create a file-sorting script that organizes files into folders based on their extensions. This practical tool is great for decluttering directories, especially downloads or workspace folders.

Project Overview

We'll create a script that:

1. Reads the contents of a directory.
2. Identifies files based on their extensions.
3. Moves files into corresponding subfolders (e.g., `.txt` files go into a "TextFiles" folder).

Requirements:

- A basic understanding of **Lua** programming.
- LuaFileSystem (`lfs`) for directory manipulation.

Step 1: Setting Up the Environment

First, ensure **Lua** and **Lua**FileSystem (`lfs`) are installed. **Lua**FileSystem is a powerful library for working with directories and files. You can install it using **Lua**Rocks:

bash

```bash
luarocks install luafilesystem
```

Step 2: Writing the Script

Complete Code

lua

```lua
-- Import the LuaFileSystem library
local lfs = require("lfs")
```

```lua
-- Function to create a
directory if it doesn't exist
local function
createDirectory(dir)

    local success, err =
lfs.mkdir(dir)

    if not success and err ~=
"File exists" then

        print("Error creating
directory:", err)

    end

end


-- Function to get the file
extension
local function
getFileExtension(filename)
```

```lua
    return
filename:match("^.+(%..+)$")
or ""

end



-- Function to sort files into
folders by extension
local                  function
sortFiles(directory)
    for        file        in
lfs.dir(directory) do
        if file ~= "." and file
~= ".." then
            local filePath =
directory .. "/" .. file
```

```lua
        local    mode    =
lfs.attributes(filePath,
"mode")


        if mode == "file"
then
            local
extension                =
getFileExtension(file):sub(2)
-- Remove the leading dot
            if   extension
~= "" then
                local
subfolder = directory .. "/" ..
extension:upper() .. "Files"

createDirectory(subfolder)  --
```

```lua
                        Create subfolder if it doesn't
exist

                                    local
newFilePath = subfolder .. "/"
.. file

os.rename(filePath,
newFilePath) -- Move the file

print("Moved:", filePath, "-
>", newFilePath)
                        end
                  end
            end
      end
end
```

```
-- Main execution

local    targetDirectory    =
"unsorted_files"    --    Replace
with your directory

print("Sorting    files    in
directory:", targetDirectory)

sortFiles(targetDirectory)

print("File            sorting
completed!")
```

Step 3: Explanation of Code

1. **Directory Handling:**
   o The createDirectory
     function ensures subfolders

are created only when
needed.

- We use `lfs.dir` to iterate
  through the files in the
  target directory.

2. **File Extension Extraction:**
   - The `getFileExtension`
     function extracts the file
     extension using a pattern
     match.

3. **Sorting Logic:**
   - Files are classified based on
     their extensions (e.g., `.txt`,
     `.png`).
   - Subfolders are named based
     on the extension category
     (e.g., "TXTFiles",
     "PNGFiles").

4. **File Movement:**
   - `os.rename` moves files
     from the original location to
     the corresponding subfolder.

Step 4: Running the Script

1. Create a directory named `unsorted_files` (or any other name, updated in `targetDirectory` in the script).
2. Populate the directory with various files (e.g., `.txt`, `.png`, `.lua`).
3. Run the script:

bash

```
lua file_sorter.lua
```

After execution, you should see subfolders like `TXTFiles`, `PNGFiles`, etc., with the respective files moved into them.

Enhancements to Explore

- **Logging**: Add a log file to record file movements.
- **Error Handling**: Handle specific cases, like duplicate file names.
- **File Type-Based Sorting**: Group files by type (e.g., "Documents" for `.txt` and `.pdf`, "Images" for `.png` and `.jpg`).
- **GUI**: Use a **Lua** GUI framework to make the script more user-friendly.

Chapter 8: Lua for Embedded Systems

Lua is widely recognized for its lightweight and efficient design, making it a favorite for embedded systems. From scripting IoT devices to controlling microcontrollers, **Lua** provides a robust yet straightforward scripting solution for hardware-level applications. In this chapter, we'll explore **Lua**'s role in embedded systems, integration with other programming languages, and debugging strategies. The hands-on project will guide you through controlling LED lights using **Lua** scripts.

8.1 Scripting IoT Devices and Microcontrollers

The Internet of Things (IoT) has revolutionized how we interact with devices, allowing seamless communication between hardware and software. **Lua** is an excellent scripting language for IoT and microcontrollers due to its lightweight design, simplicity, and flexibility. In this chapter, we'll explore how **Lua** scripts can be used to program IoT devices and microcontrollers like ESP8266 and ESP32, enabling you to control hardware and gather data effortlessly.

Why Lua for IoT and Microcontrollers?

Lua is ideal for IoT because:

- **Low Resource Usage:** Lua's minimal memory footprint is perfect for constrained environments.
- **Simplicity:** Its intuitive syntax makes it easy to write and debug scripts.
- **Portability:** **Lua** can be embedded in various IoT frameworks, like NodeMCU and Espruino.
- **Real-Time Execution:** **Lua** scripts can respond to sensor inputs or user commands with minimal latency.

Setting Up Your Microcontroller

Before diving into scripting, set up your microcontroller for **Lua** development.

1. Choose Your Microcontroller

Popular options include:

- **ESP8266**: Affordable and well-supported.
- **ESP32**: Advanced with dual-core processing and integrated Bluetooth.

2. Flash Lua Firmware

To run **Lua** scripts, flash the appropriate **Lua**-enabled firmware, such as NodeMCU, onto your microcontroller.

Steps:

1. Download NodeMCU firmware.
2. Use tools like NodeMCU PyFlasher or Esptool to flash the firmware onto the device.
3. Install a **Lua** development environment like ESPlorer.

Writing Your First Lua Script for Microcontrollers

Let's start with a simple task: blinking an LED.

Hardware Requirements

- Microcontroller (e.g., ESP8266).
- LED.
- Resistor (220 ohms).
- Breadboard and jumper wires.

Connecting the Hardware

1. Connect the LED's longer leg (anode) to GPIO pin D1 on the microcontroller.
2. Connect the shorter leg (cathode) to a resistor, then to ground.

Lua Script

lua

```lua
-- Configure GPIO pin

local pin = 1 -- GPIO pin D1

gpio.mode(pin, gpio.OUTPUT) --
Set pin as output


-- Function to toggle LED state

local function toggleLED()

    local        state        =
gpio.read(pin) -- Read current
state

    gpio.write(pin, state == 0
and gpio.HIGH or gpio.LOW) --
Toggle state

end
```

```
-- Timer to blink LED every
second

tmr.alarm(0,            1000,
tmr.ALARM_AUTO, toggleLED)
```

Explanation:

1. **Pin Configuration:** Sets GPIO pin D1 as an output pin.
2. **Toggle Function:** Reads the pin's current state and toggles it.
3. **Timer:** Calls `toggleLED` every 1,000 milliseconds (1 second).

Uploading and Running the Script

1. Use ESPlorer to upload the script.
2. Observe the LED blinking on the breadboard.

Interfacing with Sensors

Sensors play a vital role in IoT. **Lua** scripts can easily read data from sensors like temperature, humidity, or motion detectors.

Example: Reading Data from a DHT11 Temperature Sensor

Hardware Requirements:

- ESP8266 or ESP32.
- DHT11 sensor.

Circuit Connection:

1. Connect the DHT11 data pin to GPIO pin D2.
2. Connect the power and ground pins accordingly.

Lua Script:

lua

```lua
-- Load DHT module
dht = require("dht")


-- GPIO pin for the DHT11 sensor
local sensorPin = 2 -- GPIO pin D2


-- Function to read sensor data
local function readSensor()
    local status, temp, humi = dht.read(sensorPin)   -- Read data from the sensor
```

```lua
    if status == dht.OK then

print(string.format("Temperat
ure: %.1f°C", temp))

print(string.format("Humidity
: %.1f%%", humi))
    elseif       status       ==
dht.ERROR_CHECKSUM then

        print("Checksum
error.")
    elseif       status       ==
dht.ERROR_TIMEOUT then

        print("Timeout
error.")
    end
end
```

```
-- Read data every 5 seconds
tmr.alarm(1,          5000,
tmr.ALARM_AUTO, readSensor)
```

Explanation:

1. **DHT Module:** Handles the communication with the DHT11 sensor.
2. **Reading Data:** Reads temperature and humidity and prints it to the console.
3. **Timer:** Triggers the reading function every 5 seconds.

Using Wi-Fi for IoT Applications

IoT devices often communicate over Wi-Fi. **Lua** scripts can connect to a network and send data to a server or receive commands.

Connecting to a Wi-Fi Network

lua

```
-- Configure Wi-Fi in station mode

wifi.setmode(wifi.STATION)

wifi.sta.config({ssid        =
"YourSSID",          pwd       =
"YourPassword"})



-- Check connection status
```

```lua
tmr.alarm(0,                1000,
tmr.ALARM_AUTO, function()

    if wifi.sta.getip() then

        print("Connected!  IP:
" .. wifi.sta.getip())

        tmr.stop(0)

    else

print("Connecting...")

    end

end)
```

Sending Data to a Web Server

Example: Sending Sensor Data to a REST API

lua

```lua
-- HTTP module
http = require("http")


-- Function to send data
local function sendData()
    local temp = 25.5 -- Replace with actual sensor reading

    local humi = 60.0 -- Replace with actual sensor reading

    local payload = string.format('{"temperature": %.1f, "humidity": %.1f}', temp, humi)
```

```
http.post("http://example.com
/api/data",

      "Content-Type:
application/json\r\n",

      payload,

      function(code, data)

          if   code   ==   200
then

              print("Data
sent successfully!")

          else

              print("HTTP
error: " .. code)

          end

      end
```

```
    )

end


-- Send data every 10 seconds

tmr.alarm(2,          10000,
tmr.ALARM_AUTO, sendData)
```

Explanation:

1. **Wi-Fi Configuration:** Connects the microcontroller to a Wi-Fi network.
2. **HTTP Module:** Sends sensor data as a JSON payload to a REST API.

8.2 Integrating Lua with C/C++ Programs

Lua is designed to be embedded, making it a natural choice for integrating with C and C++ programs. This capability allows you to extend your existing C/C++ applications by embedding **Lua** as a scripting layer. The combination of **Lua**'s simplicity and C/C++'s performance offers a powerful toolkit for developing robust and flexible applications.

Why Integrate Lua with C/C++?

1. **Extendability**: Add scripting capabilities to your C/C++ applications without major rewrites.

2. **Flexibility:** Use **Lua** scripts to dynamically configure or control your application.
3. **Efficiency:** Combine **Lua**'s high-level abstraction with C/C++'s low-level performance.
4. **Portability: Lua**'s C-based implementation ensures compatibility with virtually any system.

Key Components of Integration

1. **Lua C API:** A set of functions provided by **Lua** for embedding and managing **Lua** states in C/C++ programs.
2. **Lua States:** The **Lua** interpreter instance that manages all **Lua** scripts and operations.

3. **Stack Mechanism:** **Lua** uses a stack-based architecture for exchanging data between **Lua** and C/C++.

Setting Up the Environment

Before diving into code, ensure you have the **Lua** development library installed.

Installing Lua Development Libraries

On   Linux:
bash

```
sudo        apt-get        install
liblua5.4-dev
```

•

On   macOS:
bash

```
brew install lua
```

-   •
-   • On Windows: Download the **Lua** binaries and development libraries from <u>lua.org</u>.

Example 1: Running Lua Code from C

In this example, we'll run a simple **Lua** script from a C program.

Lua Script (example.lua)

lua

```
-- example.lua
function greet(name)
```

```lua
    return "Hello, " .. name ..
"!"
end
```

C Code

c

```c
#include <lua.h>

#include <lualib.h>

#include <lauxlib.h>

#include <stdio.h>


int main() {
```

```c
    lua_State        *L        =
luaL_newstate(); // Create a
new Lua state

    luaL_openlibs(L);
// Open standard libraries


    // Load and execute Lua
script

    if        (luaL_dofile(L,
"example.lua") != LUA_OK) {

        fprintf(stderr,
"Error: %s\n", lua_tostring(L,
-1));

        lua_close(L);

        return 1;

    }
```

```c
    // Call the Lua function
"greet"

    lua_getglobal(L, "greet");
// Push the function onto the
stack

    lua_pushstring(L,
"World");        // Push the
argument onto the stack


    // Call the function with
1 argument and 1 return value

    if (lua_pcall(L, 1, 1, 0)
!= LUA_OK) {

        fprintf(stderr,
"Error: %s\n", lua_tostring(L,
-1));

        lua_close(L);
```

```
    return 1;

}


    // Get the return value
from the stack

    const   char   *result   =
lua_tostring(L, -1);

    printf("%s\n",    result);
// Output: Hello, World!


    lua_pop(L,              1);
// Pop the result

    lua_close(L);
// Close the Lua state

    return 0;

}
```

Explanation

1. **Lua State:** `luaL_newstate` creates a new **Lua** interpreter instance.
2. **Loading Libraries:** `luaL_openlibs` initializes standard **Lua** libraries.
3. **Script Execution:** `luaL_dofile` loads and runs the **Lua** script.
4. **Function Call:** `lua_pcall` invokes the **Lua** function `greet` with an argument from C.

Compiling and Running

Compile the C code with the **Lua** development library:

bash

```
gcc -o example example.c -llua

./example
```

Example 2: Calling C Functions from Lua

Lua can call C functions using the C API. This is useful for extending **Lua** scripts with custom functionality.

C Code

c

```
#include <lua.h>
```

```c
#include <lualib.h>

#include <lauxlib.h>

#include <stdio.h>


// A simple C function

int c_add(lua_State *L) {

    int a = lua_tointeger(L,
1); // Get the first argument

    int b = lua_tointeger(L,
2); // Get the second argument

    lua_pushinteger(L, a + b);
// Push the result onto the
stack

    return 1;                //
Return one result

}
```

```c
int main() {

    lua_State      *L      =
luaL_newstate();

    luaL_openlibs(L);


    // Register the C function
in Lua

    lua_register(L,      "add",
c_add);


    // Execute a Lua script
that calls the C function

    const    char   *script   =
"print('Result:',      add(10,
20))";
```

```
    if        (luaL_dostring(L,
script) != LUA_OK) {

        fprintf(stderr,
"Error: %s\n", lua_tostring(L,
-1));

        lua_close(L);

        return 1;

    }


    lua_close(L);

    return 0;

}
```

Explanation

1. **C Function:** `c_add` takes two integers as arguments and returns their sum.
2. **Registration:** `lua_register` makes the C function available to **Lua** scripts.
3. **Script Execution:** `luaL_dostring` runs **Lua** code directly from a string.

Output

plaintext

```
Result: 30
```

Example 3: Exchanging Complex Data

You can exchange more complex data structures, like tables, between **Lua** and C.

Lua Script (data.lua)

lua

```
-- data.lua

return {name = "Device1",
status = "active", value = 42}
```

C Code

c

```c
#include <lua.h>

#include <lualib.h>

#include <lauxlib.h>

#include <stdio.h>


int main() {

    lua_State        *L        =
luaL_newstate();

    luaL_openlibs(L);


    // Load Lua table

    if        (luaL_dofile(L,
"data.lua") != LUA_OK) {
```

```c
        fprintf(stderr,
"Error: %s\n", lua_tostring(L,
-1));

        lua_close(L);

        return 1;

    }


    // Access table fields

    lua_getfield(L,        -1,
"name");

    const    char    *name    =
lua_tostring(L, -1);

    lua_pop(L, 1);


    lua_getfield(L,        -1,
"status");
```

```c
    const    char    *status    =
lua_tostring(L, -1);

    lua_pop(L, 1);


    lua_getfield(L,            -1,
"value");

    int          value          =
lua_tointeger(L, -1);

    lua_pop(L, 1);


    // Print the values

    printf("Name:        %s\n",
name);

    printf("Status:      %s\n",
status);
```

```c
    printf("Value:        %d\n",
value);


    lua_close(L);

    return 0;

}
```

Output

plaintext

```
Name: Device1

Status: active

Value: 42
```

8.3 Debugging Embedded Scripts

Debugging embedded scripts can be challenging, especially when combining a scripting language like **Lua** with low-level programming in C/C++. However, by leveraging **Lua**'s built-in debugging tools and integrating them with external mechanisms, you can efficiently troubleshoot issues in your embedded scripts. This chapter explores the best practices, tools, and techniques to debug **Lua** scripts embedded within applications.

The Importance of Debugging Embedded Scripts

1. **Integration Complexity:** Embedding **Lua** within C/C++ applications introduces potential issues in the interaction between **Lua** scripts and host code.
2. **Script Reliability:** Debugging ensures that the scripts behave as expected under various conditions.
3. **Runtime Safety:** Identifying and resolving errors minimizes runtime crashes and undefined behavior.

Tools for Debugging Lua Scripts

1. **Lua Debug Library**
   Lua includes a debug library (debug) that provides low-level

inspection and control over **Lua**'s execution.

2. **External Debuggers**
Tools like ZeroBrane Studio or `lldb/gdb` for C/C++ enable debugging across the **Lua** and C layers.

3. **Custom Logging**
Adding logs to your **Lua** scripts and host application helps trace the execution flow.

Best Practices for Debugging Embedded Scripts

1. **Use Lua's Error Handling**: Wrap **Lua** function calls in `pcall` to capture errors without crashing the program.

2. **Enable Debug Hooks:** Use hooks to monitor function calls and executions.

3. **Separate Logic:** Modularize **Lua** scripts to isolate potential issues.

4. **Inspect Lua Stack:** Monitor the **Lua** stack for unexpected values during interactions.

Debugging Techniques

1. Using Lua's Built-In Debug Functions

The debug library provides tools to inspect the script's state and execution.

Example: Printing Variable Values

lua

```lua
local                    function
exampleFunction(a, b)

    local result = a + b

    print(debug.traceback()) -
- Prints the current stack
trace

    return result

end



exampleFunction(5, 10)
```

2. Error Handling with `pcall`

Use `pcall` (protected call) to catch
errors and prevent crashes.

C Code Example

c

```c
#include <lua.h>

#include <lualib.h>

#include <lauxlib.h>

#include <stdio.h>


int main() {

    lua_State        *L        =
luaL_newstate();

    luaL_openlibs(L);


    // Load script

    if         (luaL_dofile(L,
"script.lua") != LUA_OK) {
```

```c
        fprintf(stderr,
"Error: %s\n", lua_tostring(L,
-1));

    }


    lua_getglobal(L,
"exampleFunction");

    lua_pushnumber(L, 5);

    lua_pushnumber(L, 10);


    // Call Lua function in
protected mode

    if (lua_pcall(L, 2, 1, 0)
!= LUA_OK) {

        fprintf(stderr,
"Error: %s\n", lua_tostring(L,
-1));
```

```
    } else {

        printf("Result: %f\n",
lua_tonumber(L, -1));

    }


    lua_close(L);

    return 0;

}
```

---

3. Debugging with Hooks

Hooks allow you to track function calls, lines, or instructions during script execution.

Example: Monitoring Script Execution

lua

```lua
local function hook(event)
    print("Event: " .. event,
debug.getinfo(2,
"Sl").short_src,
debug.getinfo(2,
"l").currentline)
end


debug.sethook(hook, "crl") --
Set hook for calls, returns,
and line executions


local function testFunction()
```

```lua
    for i = 1, 5 do
        print("Count:", i)
    end
end


testFunction()
debug.sethook() -- Remove hook
```

Output:

plaintext


```
Event: call script.lua 7

Event: line script.lua 8

Count: 1
```

```
Event: line script.lua 8

Count: 2

...
```

---

4. Debugging Across Lua and C

Inspecting the Lua Stack

The **Lua** stack is central to debugging **Lua** scripts embedded in C.

Example: Inspecting Stack Values

c

```
#include <lua.h>

#include <lauxlib.h>
```

```c
#include <stdio.h>


void print_stack(lua_State *L)
{
    int top = lua_gettop(L);

    printf("Stack size: %d\n",
top);


    for (int i = 1; i <= top;
i++) {

        int t = lua_type(L,
i);

        switch (t) {

            case LUA_TSTRING:
```

```c
        printf("String:          %s\n",
        lua_tostring(L, i));

                break;

            case LUA_TNUMBER:

        printf("Number:          %g\n",
        lua_tonumber(L, i));

                break;

            case LUA_TBOOLEAN:

        printf("Boolean:         %s\n",
        lua_toboolean(L, i) ? "true" :
        "false");

                break;

            default:
```

```c
        printf("Other:          %s\n",
lua_typename(L, t));

        }

    }

}


int main() {

    lua_State      *L       =
luaL_newstate();

    luaL_openlibs(L);


    lua_pushnumber(L, 10);

    lua_pushstring(L,
"hello");
```

```
lua_pushboolean(L, 1);


print_stack(L); // Prints
stack values


lua_close(L);

return 0;

}
```

---

5. Logging Errors

Logging is crucial for embedded systems, where interactive debugging might be limited.

Example: Custom Error Logger

lua

```lua
local                function
errorHandler(err)

    local     logFile     =
io.open("error.log", "a")


logFile:write(os.date("%Y-%m-
%d %H:%M:%S") .. " - Error: "
.. err .. "\n")


logFile:write(debug.traceback
() .. "\n")

    logFile:close()
end
```

```lua
local    status,    err    =
xpcall(function()

    -- Simulated error

    error("Something    went
wrong!")

end, errorHandler)
```

Hands-On Project: Controlling LED Lights with Lua Scripts

Controlling hardware like LED lights with **Lua** scripts is an exciting way to bridge software with the physical world. This project demonstrates how to create a **Lua** script to control LEDs connected to a microcontroller such as an ESP8266 or ESP32. We'll use the NodeMCU firmware, which allows running **Lua** scripts directly on these devices.

What You'll Learn

- Setting up the hardware (microcontroller and LED).
- Writing **Lua** scripts for GPIO (General-Purpose Input/Output) control.
- Using **Lua** to create patterns and interactive controls for LEDs.

Hardware Requirements

1. ESP8266 or ESP32 microcontroller.
2. An LED.
3. A resistor (220Ω is ideal).
4. Breadboard and jumper wires.

5. USB cable to connect the microcontroller to your computer.

Software Requirements

1. NodeMCU firmware flashed onto your microcontroller.
2. A **Lua** development environment (such as ESPlorer or NodeMCU Studio).
3. Drivers for your microcontroller (CP210x or CH340).

Setting Up Your Environment

1. Flash NodeMCU Firmware

1. Download the NodeMCU firmware from the official repository.

2. Use a flashing tool (like <u>ESPTool</u>) to upload the firmware to your microcontroller.

2. Connect the Microcontroller to Your Computer

1. Plug the ESP8266/ESP32 into your computer using a USB cable.
2. Open your **Lua** development tool (e.g., ESPlorer).
3. Verify the connection by typing `print("Hello, NodeMCU!")` in the REPL (Read-Eval-Print Loop).

3. Hardware Setup

1. Connect the LED to a GPIO pin (e.g., D1 on ESP8266 or GPIO5 on ESP32).
2. Place a resistor in series with the LED to prevent overcurrent.

3. Connect the negative leg of the LED to the GND pin on the microcontroller.

Writing the Lua Script

Basic LED Control

This script demonstrates turning an LED on and off.

lua

```
-- Initialize GPIO pin

ledPin = 1 -- GPIO5 on ESP32 or
D1 on ESP8266

gpio.mode(ledPin, gpio.OUTPUT)


-- Turn LED ON
```

```
gpio.write(ledPin, gpio.HIGH)

print("LED is ON")

tmr.delay(1000000)   --   Delay
for   1   second   (1,000,000
microseconds)


-- Turn LED OFF

gpio.write(ledPin, gpio.LOW)

print("LED is OFF")
```

Explanation

1. `gpio.mode(pin, mode)`:
   Configures the specified pin as
   input or output.
2. `gpio.write(pin, state)`:
   Sets the GPIO pin to HIGH (on)
   or LOW (off).

3. `tmr.delay(time)`: Pauses execution for the specified time in microseconds.

Creating LED Blink Patterns

We can use a timer to create a blinking effect.

lua

```
-- Initialize GPIO pin

ledPin = 1

gpio.mode(ledPin, gpio.OUTPUT)
```

```lua
-- Blink LED every 500ms

tmr.create():alarm(500,
tmr.ALARM_AUTO, function()

    local    currentState    =
gpio.read(ledPin)

    gpio.write(ledPin,
currentState == gpio.HIGH and
gpio.LOW or gpio.HIGH)

end)
```

Explanation

1. `tmr.create()`: Creates a new timer object.
2. `alarm(interval, mode, callback)`: Sets the timer to trigger the callback function at specified intervals.

Interactive LED Control

This script allows you to control the LED using commands sent via the serial terminal.

lua

```lua
-- Initialize GPIO pin

ledPin = 1

gpio.mode(ledPin, gpio.OUTPUT)


-- Function to control LED

function controlLED(command)

    if command == "on" then
```

```lua
        gpio.write(ledPin,
gpio.HIGH)

        print("LED is ON")

    elseif  command  ==  "off"
then

        gpio.write(ledPin,
gpio.LOW)

        print("LED is OFF")

    else

        print("Unknown
command. Use 'on' or 'off'.")

    end

end


-- Listen for user input
```

```lua
uart.on("data",            "\n",
function(data)


controlLED(data:match("^%s*(.
-)%s*$")) -- Trim whitespace
and pass command

end, 0)
```

How to Use

1. Open the serial terminal in your **Lua** development tool.
2. Type on to turn the LED on or off to turn it off.

Advanced: LED Patterns with Functions

Create complex patterns like a breathing LED effect.

lua

```lua
-- Initialize GPIO pin
ledPin = 1
gpio.mode(ledPin, gpio.OUTPUT)


-- Create a breathing LED
effect
local pwm = require("pwm")


pwm.setup(ledPin, 1000, 0) --
1 kHz frequency, duty cycle 0%
pwm.start(ledPin)


local duty = 0
```

```lua
local increment = 5


tmr.create():alarm(50,
tmr.ALARM_AUTO, function()

    duty = duty + increment

    if duty >= 1023 or duty <=
0 then

        increment = -increment

    end

    pwm.setduty(ledPin, duty)

end)
```

Explanation

1. `pwm.setup(pin, frequency, duty)`: Configures a PWM signal on the pin.
2. `pwm.setduty(pin, duty)`: Adjusts the duty cycle to control brightness.
3. A timer smoothly increases and decreases the duty cycle for a breathing effect.

Lua's flexibility and lightweight nature make it an excellent choice for embedded systems and IoT projects. From basic GPIO control to integrating with C programs, **Lua** bridges the gap between high-level scripting and low-level hardware manipulation. This chapter has equipped you with foundational knowledge and practical skills to use **Lua** effectively in embedded systems development.

Chapter 9: Debugging and Performance Optimization

Debugging and performance optimization are critical skills for every **Lua** developer. They ensure your scripts run efficiently and behave as expected. This chapter introduces debugging tools and techniques, profiling to identify performance bottlenecks, and strategies for robust error handling.

9.1 Debugging Tools and Techniques

Debugging is the process of identifying and fixing issues in your **Lua** scripts. **Lua** provides several built-in tools and practices to streamline debugging.

Using `print` Statements

The simplest debugging method involves strategically placing `print` statements to monitor variable values and program flow.

lua

```lua
local function addNumbers(a, b)
    print("Input values:", a, b) -- Debugging print
    return a + b
end


local result = addNumbers(3, 5)
```

```lua
print("Result:", result)
```

Error Functions

Lua offers the `error` and `assert` functions to generate errors when unexpected situations occur.

- `error(message)`: Stops execution and displays an error message.
- `assert(condition, message)`: Checks a condition; if false, raises an error with the specified message.

lua

```lua
local function divide(a, b)
```

```lua
    assert(b ~= 0, "Division
by zero is not allowed")

    return a / b

end


print(divide(10, 2))  -- Works

print(divide(10,   0))       --
Triggers an error
```

Using the debug Library

Lua's debug library provides tools for inspecting and controlling the execution of Lua code. Commonly used functions include:

- **debug.traceback([message], [level])**: Generates a stack trace.

- **debug.getinfo(function)**: Retrieves function details.

lua

```lua
local                    function
faultyFunction()

    local x = 10 / 0    --
Intentional error

end


local success, message =
pcall(faultyFunction)

if not success then

    print("Error occurred: ",
message)
```

```lua
    print("Stack    trace:    ",
debug.traceback())

end
```

9.2 Profiling and Improving Performance

Profiling involves analyzing your code's performance to identify bottlenecks and optimize execution speed.

Measuring Execution Time

Use `os.clock` to measure the execution time of specific code sections.

lua

```lua
local startTime = os.clock()
```

```lua
-- Code block to test

local sum = 0

for i = 1, 1e6 do

    sum = sum + i

end


local endTime = os.clock()

print("Execution        time:",
endTime - startTime)
```

Optimization Techniques

1. **Precompute Values:** Avoid recalculating the same result repeatedly.

469

2. **Table Management:** Reuse tables instead of creating new ones.
3. **Reduce Global Lookups:** Store frequently accessed globals in local variables.

9.3 Error Handling Strategies

Proper error handling improves the reliability of your **Lua** applications.

Using `pcall` and `xpcall`

- `pcall` **(protected call):** Executes a function and catches errors.
- `xpcall`: Similar to `pcall` but allows custom error handling functions.

lua

```lua
local                function
riskyOperation()
    error("Something        went
wrong")
end


local   success,   message   =
pcall(riskyOperation)
if not success then
    print("Error      handled:",
message)
end
```

Custom Error Handling with xpcall

lua

```lua
local                function
errorHandler(err)

    return "Handled error: "
.. err

end


local                function
riskyOperation()

    error("Critical failure")

end


local success, message =
xpcall(riskyOperation,
errorHandler)

if not success then
```

```lua
    print(message)

end
```

Hands-On Project: Debugging and Optimizing a Game Script

In this project, you'll debug and optimize a simple game script to enhance performance and reliability.

Step 1: The Initial Script

Here's a basic game simulation with bugs and inefficiencies:

lua

```lua
local game = {
```

473

```lua
    score = 0,

    enemies    =    {"enemy1",
"enemy2", "enemy3"},

}


function game:addScore(points)

    self.score = self.score +
points

end


function
game:removeEnemy(name)

    for    i,    enemy    in
ipairs(self.enemies) do

        if enemy == name then
```

```lua
        table.remove(self.enemies, i)

        end

    end

end


-- Simulate gameplay

game:addScore(10)

game:removeEnemy("enemy2")

print("Score:", game.score)

print("Enemies    remaining:",
#game.enemies)
```

Step 2: Debugging Issues

- Verify functionality using print.

- Add error checks for missing
  enemies during removal.

lua

```lua
function
game:removeEnemy(name)

    local found = false

    for    i,    enemy    in
ipairs(self.enemies) do

        if enemy == name then

table.remove(self.enemies, i)

            found = true

        end

    end

    if not found then
```

```lua
        print("Error:    Enemy
not found:", name)

    end

end
```

Step 3: Optimizing the Script

- Avoid repeated table scans by
  exiting the loop early.

lua

```lua
function
game:removeEnemy(name)

    for    i,    enemy    in
ipairs(self.enemies) do

        if enemy == name then
```

```lua
        table.remove(self.enemies, i)

            return    -- Exit
after finding the enemy

        end

    end

    print("Error:  Enemy  not
found:", name)

end
```

Debugging and performance optimization are essential for creating efficient and error-free **Lua** scripts. With these tools and techniques, you can confidently tackle errors, enhance execution speed, and build robust **Lua** applications.

Chapter 10: Expanding Lua's Capabilities

Lua is highly versatile, with the ability to integrate with external libraries, serve as an embedded language in larger applications, and power various game engines. In this chapter, we explore how to extend **Lua**'s functionality, embed it into complex applications, and utilize it in popular game development environments.

10.1 Using External Libraries and Extensions

External libraries enhance **Lua**'s core functionality by adding specialized features or simplifying complex tasks.

Installing Libraries with LuaRocks

LuaRocks is the go-to package manager for **Lua**. It allows you to install, manage, and remove libraries with ease.

Steps to Install LuaRocks:

1. Download and install **LuaRocks** from its official website.
2. Use the `luarocks install` command to install libraries.

Example: Installing the `luasocket` library for network programming.

bash

```
luarocks install luasocket
```

Using Installed Libraries

To use a library, simply require it in your script.

lua

```
local socket = require("socket")


-- Get the current time from an online server
local client = socket.tcp()
client:connect("time.nist.gov", 13)
```

```lua
local        response        =
client:receive("*a")

print("Current        Time:",
response)

client:close()
```

Creating Custom Extensions

You can write custom **Lua** modules to encapsulate reusable code.

lua

```lua
-- File: mymodule.lua
local mymodule = {}


function mymodule.greet(name)
```

```lua
    return "Hello, " .. name ..
"!"

end


return mymodule
```

Usage:

lua

```lua
local          mymodule          =
require("mymodule")

print(mymodule.greet("Alice")
)
```

10.2 Embedding Lua in Larger Applications

Embedding **Lua** into larger applications allows developers to use it as a scripting engine. This is particularly useful for applications requiring dynamic configurations or user customizations.

Embedding Lua in C Applications

The **Lua** C API provides functions to embed **Lua** into C programs.

Basic Example: Executing **Lua** code from C.

c

```c
#include <lua.h>

#include <lualib.h>

#include <lauxlib.h>
```

```c
int main() {

    lua_State      *L      = luaL_newstate();   // Create a new Lua state

    luaL_openlibs(L);
// Load standard libraries


    // Execute a Lua script

    luaL_dostring(L,
"print('Hello from Lua!')");


    lua_close(L);
// Close Lua state

    return 0;

}
```

Calling Lua Functions from C

c

```c
#include <lua.h>

#include <lualib.h>

#include <lauxlib.h>


int main() {
    lua_State        *L        =
luaL_newstate();

    luaL_openlibs(L);


    // Load and execute Lua
script
```

```
luaL_dofile(L,
"script.lua");


// Call Lua function

lua_getglobal(L,
"addNumbers");       //      Push
function to stack

lua_pushnumber(L,       5);
// Push first argument

lua_pushnumber(L,      10);
// Push second argument

lua_call(L,      2,      1);
// Call  function (2  args,  1
result)
```

```c
    int        result        =
lua_tonumber(L,  -1);  // Get
result

    printf("Result:      %d\n",
result);


    lua_close(L);

    return 0;

}
```

10.3 Lua in Game Engines

Lua is widely used in game engines for scripting. Here, we focus on three popular engines: Unity, Roblox, and Corona SDK.

Lua with Unity

Unity integrates **Lua** via third-party libraries like MoonSharp. MoonSharp allows developers to use **Lua** for scripting game logic.

Example: Scripting in **Lua** with MoonSharp.

lua

```lua
-- Unity script file with MoonSharp

local player = {health = 100}


function takeDamage(damage)
    player.health = player.health - damage
```

```
    return player.health

end
```

Lua with Roblox

Roblox uses **Lua** as its primary scripting language, allowing developers to create immersive experiences.

Example: Basic Roblox **Lua** Script.

lua

```
local          part           =
Instance.new("Part")

part.Size = Vector3.new(4, 1,
2)

part.Position = Vector3.new(0,
10, 0)
```

```
part.Anchored = true

part.Parent = game.Workspace
```

Lua with Corona SDK

Corona SDK is a lightweight framework for 2D games that relies on **Lua** for scripting.

Example: A basic scene setup in Corona.

lua

```
local          rect          =
display.newRect(100, 100, 50,
50)

rect:setFillColor(1, 0, 0)


function rect:touch(event)
```

```
    if event.phase == "began"
then

        print("Rectangle
touched!")

    end

    return true

end


rect:addEventListener("touch"
, rect)
```

Hands-On Project: Creating a Basic Platformer Game

Objective

Develop a simple platformer game using **Lua** and Love2D, featuring a player, platforms, and basic physics.

Step 1: Setting Up the Environment

Create a `main.lua` file and initialize Love2D.

lua

```
function love.load()
    player = {x = 50, y = 300,
width = 20, height = 40, speed
```

```lua
= 200, jumpPower = -300, dy =
0, onGround = false}

    platforms = {{x = 0, y =
350, width = 800, height = 20}}

end
```

Step 2: Drawing the Game

Render the player and platforms.

lua

```lua
function love.draw()

    love.graphics.setColor(1,
0, 0)


love.graphics.rectangle("fill
```

```lua
",    player.x,    player.y,
player.width, player.height)


    love.graphics.setColor(0,
1, 0)
    for    _,    platform    in
ipairs(platforms) do

love.graphics.rectangle("fill
",    platform.x,    platform.y,
platform.width,
platform.height)
    end
end
```

Step 3: Adding Physics

Implement player movement and jumping.

lua

```lua
function love.update(dt)

    player.dy = player.dy +
(500 * dt) -- Gravity


    if
love.keyboard.isDown("right")
then

        player.x = player.x +
player.speed * dt

    elseif
love.keyboard.isDown("left")
then
```

```lua
        player.x = player.x -
player.speed * dt

    end


    -- Jump

    if
love.keyboard.isDown("space")
and player.onGround then

        player.dy          =
player.jumpPower

        player.onGround    =
false

    end


    player.y   =   player.y   +
player.dy   *   dt   --   Apply
vertical movement
```

```lua
    -- Collision detection

    for    _,    platform    in
ipairs(platforms) do

        if       player.y       +
player.height > platform.y and

            player.x            +
player.width > platform.x and

            player.x            <
platform.x  +  platform.width
then

            player.y          =
platform.y - player.height

            player.dy = 0

            player.onGround   =
true

        end
```

```
        end

end
```

Step 4: Enhancements

- Add collectibles or enemies.
- Use animations for player movement.

This chapter explored **Lua**'s extended capabilities with libraries, embedding, and game engines. The hands-on project demonstrated how **Lua** could be used to build a functional platformer, equipping you with skills to create more complex applications.

Appendices

Appendix A: Lua Quick Reference Guide

This quick reference guide provides an overview of essential **Lua** syntax and functionality to help you quickly find and recall key concepts.

Basic Syntax

lua

```lua
-- Single-line comment
--[[
    Multi-line comment
]]
```

```lua
-- Variables

local x = 10      -- Local variable

global_y = 20     -- Global variable


-- Data types: nil, boolean, number, string, table, function

print(type(x))    -- Output: number
```

Control Structures

lua

```lua
-- If-Else
```

```lua
if x > 5 then
    print("x is greater than 5")
else
    print("x is 5 or less")
end


-- Loops
for i = 1, 10 do
    print(i)
end


local i = 0
while i < 10 do
```

```lua
    print(i)

    i = i + 1

end
```

Functions

lua

```lua
function add(a, b)

    return a + b

end

print(add(5, 10))   -- Output:
15


-- Anonymous function
```

```lua
local multiply = function(a, b)
    return a * b
end
```

Tables

lua

```lua
-- Tables as arrays
local fruits = {"apple", "banana", "cherry"}
print(fruits[1])    -- Output: apple


-- Tables as dictionaries
```

```lua
local person = {name = "Alice",
age = 25}

print(person.name)  -- Output:
Alice



-- Adding to a table

table.insert(fruits, "date")
```

Appendix B: Troubleshooting Common Errors

1. Syntax Errors

Error: `unexpected symbol near 'x'`
Cause: A typo or misplaced symbol in your code.

Solution: Check for missing or extra characters like = or `end`.

2. Nil Value Access

Error: `attempt to index a nil value`

Cause: Accessing a non-existent key in a table or using a variable before initialization.

Solution: Verify table keys or ensure the variable is initialized.

3. Type Mismatch

Error: `attempt to concatenate a number value`

Cause: Using mismatched types, such as combining strings and numbers.

Solution: Convert types explicitly using `tostring()` or `tonumber()`.

4. Infinite Loops

Error: High CPU usage or non-responsive program.

Cause: A loop with no exit condition.

Solution: Add proper exit conditions to your loops.

Appendix C: Sample Scripts and Templates

1. Hello World

lua

```
print("Hello, World!")
```

2. File Reading and Writing

lua

```
-- Writing to a file
```

```lua
local          file          =
io.open("example.txt", "w")

file:write("Hello, Lua!")

file:close()


-- Reading from a file

file = io.open("example.txt",
"r")

local          content          =
file:read("*a")

print(content)

file:close()
```

3. Simple HTTP Request (with LuaSocket)

lua

```lua
local          http          =
require("socket.http")

local          response          =
http.request("http://example.
com")

print(response)
```

4. Basic Timer

lua

```lua
local start = os.time()

while os.time() - start < 5 do

    print("Waiting...")

    os.execute("sleep 1")

end
```

```lua
print("5 seconds passed!")
```

5. Game Loop Template (Love2D)

lua

```lua
function love.load()
    player = {x = 50, y = 50,
speed = 200}
end



function love.update(dt)
    if
love.keyboard.isDown("up")
then
        player.y = player.y -
player.speed * dt
```

```lua
    elseif
love.keyboard.isDown("down")
then

        player.y = player.y +
player.speed * dt

    end

end


function love.draw()

love.graphics.rectangle("fill
", player.x, player.y, 50, 50)

end
```

This appendix provides the essential tools, guidance, and examples for quick implementation and troubleshooting in **Lua** development projects.

www.ingramcontent.com/pod-product-compliance
Lightning Source LLC
La Vergne TN
LVHW022332060326
832902LV00022B/3999